Frank Milton Bristol

Richard The Third And The Primrose Criticism

Frank Milton Bristol

Richard The Third And The Primrose Criticism

ISBN/EAN: 9783741186462

Manufactured in Europe, USA, Canada, Australia, Japa

Cover: Foto ©ninafisch / pixelio.de

Manufactured and distributed by brebook publishing software (www.brebook.com)

Frank Milton Bristol

Richard The Third And The Primrose Criticism

Richard the Third

AND

The Primrose Criticism

"A primrose by the river's brim
A yellow primrose was to him,
And it was nothing more."

CHICAGO
A. C. McCLURG AND COMPANY
1887

COPYRIGHT,
BY A. C. MCCLURG AND CO.,
A.D. 1887.

I ASK you to listen to a few words: first, a few general remarks on criticism, and then an illustration of them from the play of 'Richard III.,' or rather from the absence of certain things in the play of 'Richard III.,' which, to my mind, seem to indicate that it is not Shakespeare's work.

I propose to say a few words on one of the plays usually attributed to him, — a play in respect of which I find myself in the position of poor Peter Bell, seeing little more than an ordinary primrose where I perhaps hoped to see a plant, a flower of light. I mean the play of 'Richard III.'

JAMES RUSSELL LOWELL,
Chicago, Feb. 22, 1887.

CONTENTS.

Part I.
THE PRIMROSE CRITICISM . . . . . PAGE 11

Part II.
THE HISTORICAL BASIS OF RICHARD III. 65

Part III.
THE HISTRIONIC RICHARDS 109

PART I.

THE PRIMROSE CRITICISM.

"Your reasons are too shallow and too quick."

THE PRIMROSE CRITICISM.

"THE pale primroses,
That die unmarried ere they can behold
Bright Phœbus in his strength,"

may have contained virtues of beauty and suggestion which escaped the peculiar eye of Peter Bell. There may have been a language in them which to other eyes revealed ideas of taste, design, wisdom, creation. To Peter Bell and his Primrose Criticism many another object of beauty in nature, art, and literature has appeared to be but commonplace, though it bore the impress of high origin, and carried in upon other minds exquisite sentiments and edifying speculations. The historical tragedy of 'Richard III.' excites no admiration in the common-sense mind of Peter Bell. He fails to discover its poetic and dramatic merits, but, more particularly, seems to be oblivious to those masterly touches of energy and grandeur which declare its author to be Shakespeare. Primrose Criticism assumes to be synonymous with Common Sense, which is the only safe guide in the study of any subject, whether it be the Primrose or 'Richard the Third.' It is to be regretted, however, that Peter Bell has been so backward in coming forward with his peculiar critical method; and that, as a consequence, the world has been studying the "thousand-souled" Shakespeare for three hundred years without the light of common-sense. So uncommon was the sense of Pope, Dryden, rare Ben Jonson, and "starry-minded" Milton, the poet-eulogists of our glorious bard, that they accepted base counterfeits for the genuine productions of his inspired pen! So uncommon were the sense and scholarship of the distinguished commentators and editors, — Rowe, Farmer, Theobald, Capell, Hanmer, Steevens, Johnson, Malone, Chalmers, Douce, Dyce, and Knight, — that they were unable, with a life-long study, to distinguish between the genuine and the spurious plays of Shakespeare! With their masterful knowledge of Elizabethan literature, and their familiar acquaintance with the English dramatists, they do not seem to have had the slightest suspicion that 'Richard III.' was not written in the style of Shakespeare, or that it was unworthy of him and must have been the production of an inferior genius.

Alas, that Peter Bell should have been so tardy in making his appearance! But Primrose Criticism had to await the coming of Peter Bell, and Peter Bell the advent of Wordsworth. It is certainly only a coincidence; but Peter Bell's criticism of the Primrose was almost identical with Wordsworth's estimate of Shakespeare. The author of 'Peter Bell' should not blame poor Peter for a dulness of vision of which he is himself guilty. On the authority of Mr. Buckle, Wordsworth once told Charles Lamb that Shakespeare was not so great as he was popularly estimated to be, and thought that he could, if he had a mind, write as well as Shakespeare. "But then, you see," said Lamb, "he had not the *mind.*" Wordsworth looked upon Shakespeare through the very spectacles of Peter Bell, and

> The primrose by the *Avon's* brim
> A yellow primrose was to him,
> And it was nothing more.

But to all eyes that wear not Peter Bell's spectacles the world never grew, before nor since, such another primrose.

"Beware (delighted Poets!) when you sing
  To welcome Nature in the early Spring:
    Your num'rous Feet not tread
    The Banks of Avon; for each Flowre
    (As it nere knew a Sunne or Showre)
      Hangs there, the pensive head.

"Each Tree, whose thick, and spreading growth hath made
  Rather a Night beneath the Boughs than shade,
    (Unwilling now to grow.)
    Lookes like a Plume a Captaine weares,
    Whose rifled Falls are steept i' th teares
      Which from his last rage flow.

"The pitious River wept it selfe away
  Long since (Alas!) to such a swift decay;
    That reach the Map, and looke
    If you a River there can spie;
    And for a River your mock'd Eye,
      Will find a shallow Brooke."

Valuable as common-sense may be, possibly the sense of man should not grow too common, if it would appreciate the most uncommon sense that ever yet was writ. Let it be admitted, however, that the unadulterated Primrose Criticism fully appreciates Shakespeare's genius, and even places him far above the ignoble possibility of errors and vulgar faults; yet it attempts to stab to the heart the most celebrated offspring of the poet's genius, and then to deny its Shakespearian legitimacy.

It is to be supposed that a shoemaker is the best judge of a shoe, an artist of a picture, and a poet of verse. But while the cobbler's judgment as to the quality of the shoe must be accepted, the soundness of his judgment as to the age and the maker of it may be questioned. The poet may pass judgment on the poetical merits of an 'Iliad,' 'The Faerie Queene,' or a 'Richard III.,' but his poetical genius and instinct alone are not sufficient foundation for a judgment that must rest on historical data, on antiquarian knowledge, on records, facts, and logic. Let the poet declare on his judgment that 'Richard III.' is an inferior production, — that it by merit holds no high rank among dramas. Then let the critic have the courage of a Voltaire or a Wordsworth and attack Shakespeare himself, — point out his faults, expose his blunders, and show wherein his genius has been overrated. Here is critical heroism and enterprise. When Peter Bell turned his unique optics upon the primrose, and stared in upon its delicate beauty, he did not have the temerity to argue that as the primrose is nothing but a primrose, therefore the Almighty needs to be relieved of the responsibility of having created it. But Peter Bell grows brave as he scrutinizes the dramatic flower known as 'Richard III.' To his superb common-sense it is but a rank and unsightly weed of low and vulgar origin. "But, 'in the name of all the gods at once,' charge me not," says Peter, "with the unpardonable offence of imputing any fault or slightest imperfection to Shakespeare's infallible judgment and genius, because 'Richard III.,' you know, must not be attributed to his divine, unerring pen." Sublime critical courage! Marvellous veneration for Shakespeare!

The Primrose Criticism lays down the new canon that whatever a genius may do that is unworthy of him shall not be attributed to him, but shall be branded as a literary foundling. Happy the artist, general, statesman, historian, preacher, or poet who may be thus easily relieved of responsibility for his faults and weaknesses! But is this Common-sense Criticism? It is undoubtedly Primrose-sense, and Peter-Bell-sense put to criticism; but, in the name of scientific and literary integrity, let it be hoped that it will long remain very Uncommon-sense.

The arguments employed by the Primrose Criticism in its attempt to rob Shakespeare of 'Richard III.' are not sound. One argument stands in this shape : Shakespeare never wrote deliberate nonsense, nor knowingly indulged in defective metre. 'Richard III.' contains deliberate nonsense and premeditated defective metre. Ergo : Shakespeare never wrote the historical tragedy of 'Richard III.' With all due and unfeigned respect for him who advanced this argument, it cannot be accepted as sound and reliable. It suggests itself to a careful student of the Primrose method, that it would take very uncommon sense at this time to discover whether Shakespeare's nonsense was deliberate or not, and whether he indulged in defective metre knowingly or unknowingly. The discussion of questions of this character is as futile as it is unimportant. But if Primrose Criticism affirms that Shakespeare never wrote nonsense nor indulged in defective metre as a fact, there shall be a square issue, which may be settled without resort to any transcendental speculations. Shakespeare did write nonsense, and he indulged very frequently in defective metre. Peter Bell must be developing a supernatural power of vision in these latter days that he is able to discover in every production of Shakespeare absolute perfection of poetical form, infallibility of dramatic plan, unadulterated wisdom, and impeccable fancy. Surely this is finding "infinite deeps and marvellous revelations in a primrose."

There is not a play, among all that are attributed to Shakespeare, which can be said to be absolutely free from nonsense. Nor is there a single play that is absolutely free from defective metre. These are the very faults which our poet's detractors have most successfully proven against him, and which his admirers have most unhesitatingly admitted. Rare Ben Jonson was almost prophetic in his honest criticism; writing, it would seem, with his eye on the Primrose critic of this far-off time. "I remember," says he, "the Players have often mentioned it as an honor to Shakespeare, that in his writing (whatsoever he penn'd) hee never blotted out line. My answer hath beene, would he had blotted a thousand. Which they thought a malevolent speech. I had not told posterity this, but for their ignorance, who choose that circumstance to commend their friend by, wherein

THE PRIMROSE CRITICISM. 19

he most faulted." Editors and commentators have been severely and justly criticised themselves for attempting to correct Shakespeare's nonsense and defective metre. The perfection of nonsense has been employed to explain away the nonsense of Shakespeare; syllables have been added to or subtracted from his lines, and absolute prose changed into verse to mend the poet's limping metre. But the best editions of Shakespeare's works at the present time contain, in almost if not quite every play, instances of nonsense and of defective metre which have fortunately been rescued from the literary botchery of over-nice emendators whose delicate tastes and sensitive ears could not permit Shakespeare's art to remain in its original and now valuable imperfection. It is the aim of the highest Shakespearian scholarship and editorship to permit this age and all the future to know what this singer really sang, and to let

"sweetest Shakespeare, Fancy's child,
Warble his native wood-notes wild."

The metrical dissonance of an Alexandrine or a blank prose line introduced into the harmony of heroic verse has often thrown such critics as Steevens, Seymour, and Collier into the very anguish of hypercriticism and into those emendatory spasms that have resulted in the infliction of wounds of metrical corrections upon the original text of Shakespeare's plays, which the best and wisest scholarship of to-day would heal and obliterate.

Primrose Criticism affirms that the original text of Shakespeare's plays could not have contained a faulty verse, nor a passage of obscure sense, nor a low, unchaste fancy. The conclusion is, that every such defect must be an interpolation, which originated with actors, short-hand reporters, and brainless critics of the Anti-Primrose school. This is certainly a *petitio principii*, if we are to ignore all the historical and scientific data on which an argument for the genuineness of the text should be based.

The scholarly judgment of Richard Grant White had not been bewitched by the Primrose method when he wrote: "Not what Shakespeare might, could, would, or should have written, but what, according to the best evidence, did he write, is the only admissible or defensible object of the labors of his editors and verbal critics." This is true common-sense applied to the study of Shakespeare; and no critic need fear that he will be "laying himself open to the reproach of applying common sense to the study of Shakespeare," who tramples upon this canon. It may require an uncommon sense to determine what Shakespeare might, could, would, or should have written, — and this the Primrose Criticism, in consistency, should never attempt, — but to determine what Shakespeare did write may require simply that ordinary common-sense which is to be distinguished from extraordinary Primrose common-sense.

The external evidences of the Shakespearian authorship of 'Richard III.' are many and indisputable.

In the Books of the Stationers' Company, London, the play is attributed to Shakespeare. Four editions of the quarto were issued during the author's lifetime. The first edition was published in 1597, according to the Stationers' Registers. This first edition did not bear the name of its author. It was published anonymously. All the subsequent editions, 1598, 1602, 1605, 1612, 1621, 1622, 1629, and 1634, bore the name of William Shakespeare. When Shakespeare's complete plays were first published, in 1623, 'Richard III.' was included. Nor has that play ever been excluded from the undisputed works of Shakespeare.

This is at least *prima facie* evidence of the Shakespearian authorship of the play. If it be argued that some doubt is justified by the absence of Shakespeare's name from the title-page of the first quarto edition, the reply will be, that on the same ground doubt should be cast on the Shakespearian authorship of 'Richard II.,' 'Romeo and Juliet,' 'Henry IV.,' and 'Henry V.,' which even Primrose Criticism may not be prepared to do. At least three editions of 'Richard III.' were published during the lifetime of the author, bearing his name, nor was any question then raised as to the genuineness of the play. After the author's death, as has been stated, this tragedy took its place in all the folio editions of Shakespeare's works, and has not in a single instance been denied its rightful place in subsequent editions.

It is not altogether unimportant as an argument, that this play has passed without challenge the scholarly and critical scrutiny of Rowe, Pope, Theobald, Hanmer, Warburton, Johnson, Capell, Steevens, Reed, Malone, Chalmers, Harness, Singer, Knight, Collier, Halliwell-Phillipps, Hudson, Dyce, White, and Clarke, — a score of editors and critics whose several and united scholarship is the pride and glory of English letters. It will take a more vigorous logic than Primrose Criticism employs to set aside the verdict of this splendid array of scholars.

It may strengthen the confidence of the wavering to glance at some of the allusions made to Shakespeare in connection with the play of 'Richard III.' by contemporaneous and immediately succeeding poets. There does not seem to have been a suspicion in Shakespeare's day that he was not the author of this tragedy, or that he had perpetrated the literary fraud of putting his name to a drama which he did not write.

One of the earliest references to Shakespeare is made in John Weever's Poem (1599), *Ad Gulielmum Shakespeare*.

" Honie-Tong'd *Shakespeare* when I saw thine issue
I swore *Apollo* got them and none other."

Of this " issue," the poet mentions " Rose-checkt *Adonis*," " Faire fire-hot *Venus*," " Chaste *Lucretia*," and

" *Romeo-Richard;* more whose names I know not."

Francis Meres, in his 'Palladis Tamia,' 1598, refers to Shakespeare in the words :—

" As Plautus and Seneca are accounted the best for Comedy and Tragedy among the

Latins; so Shakespeare among ye English is the most excellent in both kinds of the stage . . . witness . . . for Tragedy his Richard the 2, Richard the 3, Henry the 4, King John, Titus Andronicus and his Romeo and Juliet."

There was a rather broad anecdote current in Shakespeare's time, in which both the poet's and the actor Burbage's names were associated with the name and play of 'Richard III.,' which would be out of character here. But this same Burbage, Shakespeare's friend and the original Richard, is introduced as one of the characters in a play entitled 'The Returne from Pernassus; or the Scourge of Simony, publiquely acted by the Students in St. John's College in Camebridge, 1606.' The following lines occur in this play : —

"*Kemp.* Few of the university pen plaies well, they smell too much of that writer *Ovid*, and that writer *Metamorphosis*, and talke too much of *Proserpina* & *Juppiter*. Why here 's our fellow *Shakespeare* puts them all downe, I, and *Ben Jonson*, too. O, that *Ben Jonson* is a pestilent fellow, he brought up *Horace* giving the Poets a pill, but our fellow *Shakespeare* hath given him a purge that made him beray his credit.

. . . .

Burbage. I like your face, and the proportion of your body for Richard the 3. I pray, M. Phil. let me see you act a little of it.

Philo. Now is the winter of our discontent,
Made glorious summer by this sonne of Yorke," etc·

In a religious poem on 'Saint Mary Magdalen's Conversion,' written by 'C. J.,' 1603; the following lines occur :—

" Of *Helens* rape and *Troyes* besieged Towne,
Of Troylus faith, and *Cressids* falsitie,
Of *Richards* stratagems for the english crowne,
Of *Tarquins* lust, and Lucrece chastitie,
Of these, of none of these my muse now treates,
Of greater conquests, warres and loves she speakes."

Richard Brathwaite, in 'A Strappado for the Devill,' 1615, writes the lines :—

"If I had liv'd but in King Richard's days,
Who in his heat of passion, midst the force
Of his assailants troubled many waies,
Crying A horse, a kingdome for a horse,
O! then my horse, which now at livery stayes,
Had beene set free, where now he's forc't to stand,
And like to fall into the Ostler's hand."

If it be kept in mind that these allusions to Shakespeare and his 'Richard III.' were made in his own lifetime and during the time in which Burbage was gaining celebrity as the principal character in the tragedy, the statement that Shakespeare was credited with the authorship of 'Richard III.,' and that this tragedy produced a deep impression on literary as well as vulgar minds, will be admitted.

John Milton was one of Shakespeare's most enthusiastic eulogists, and, beyond question, an ardent student of his works. It would be remarkable for him to have given special attention to 'Richard III.' without discovering that it was written in a style wholly foreign to the manner of Shakespeare, if such were the case. It is matter for wonder that Milton's poetic tastes, instincts, and judgment did not equal the Primrose sense of Peter Bell in detecting the un-Shakespearian character of that tragedy. It is still more surprising, if the play is so very commonplace and is not the production of Shakespeare's genius, that glorious John Milton should have found in that very play some of the most striking ideas which he has introduced into 'Paradise Lost,' and that he should have quoted from that very play in his prose works, where he attributes the play to Shakespeare. Sir William Blackstone and Edmund Malone could not but think that Milton was indebted for his characterization of Satan to these lines: —

"Sin, death, and hell have set their marks on him;
And all their ministers attend on him."
ACT I. *Scene* 3.

In 'Eikonoklastes,' written in answer to 'Eikon Basilike,' in 1690, Milton makes this striking reference to Shakespeare and the play of 'Richard III.:'—

"From Stories of this nature both Ancient and Modern which abound, the Poets also, and some English, have been in this Point so mindful of *Decorum*, as to put never more pious words in the Mouth of any Person, than of a Tyrant. I shall not instance an abstruse Author, wherein the King may be less conversant, but one whom we well know was the Closet Companion of these his Solitudes, *William Shakespeare;* who introduces the Person of *Richard* the Third, speaking, in as high a strain of Piety, and mortification, as is uttered in any passage of this Book and sometimes to the same sense and purpose with some words in this Place, I *intended,* saith he, *not only to oblige my Friends, but mine enemies.* The like saith *Richard, Act* II. *Scene* 1:—

'*I do not know that English Man alive,*
With whom my soul is any jot at odds,
More than the Infant that is born to-night;
I thank my God for my humility.'

"Other stuff of this sort may be read throughout the whole Tragedy, wherein the Poet us'd not much License in departing from the Truth of History, which delivers him a deep Dissembler, not of his affections only, but of Religion."

As the great poets themselves, including Jonson, Milton, Dryden, and Pope, never questioned the Shakespearian authorship of 'Richard III.,' so the great actors who have won their renown in Shakespearian characters, and who have made Richard III. one of the most celebrated histrionic representations of the English stage, have never detected that Richard was not Shakespeare's. Burbage, Ryan, Cibber, Garrick, Mossop, Henderson, Cooke, Kean, Kemble, Booth, Macready — all the great, original Richards — have had as firm confidence in the Shakespearian authorship of this character as they have had of Hamlet, Macbeth, Coriolanus, Othello, Shylock, or Lear. It is ordinarily, if not extraordinarily reasonable, to suppose that actors of such intelligence and genius, actors devoted to the study and representation of Shakespeare, would be able to detect, if it existed, the un-Shakespearian character of 'Richard III.' The universal opinion of the stage is not easily to be set aside by the Primrose Criticism. Peter Bell has not a more authoritative voice than Burbage, Betterton, Cibber, Garrick, Kemble, Cooke, Kean, Young, and Macready.

The judgment of learned and philosophical students of Shakespeare should not be ignored in a discussion of this character. Yet Primrose Criticism is peculiarly and significantly hostile to anything that approaches the uncommon in sense, learning, scholarship, or subtlety of criticism; hence its antipathy to German criticism, and the scientific, philosophical instincts of the German mind. There may be method in this madness when Shakespeare is under discussion, as it is beyond all dispute that the Germans are the broadest, profoundest, and most scholarly critics and commentators of Shakespeare in the world. Englishmen must admit this, as the able and candid Furnivall has done. Lessing, Goethe, Schiller, Tieck, Schlegel, Ulrici, and Gervinus are names that cannot be cast into shadow by even such names as Pope, Dryden, Johnson, Malone, Steevens, Collier, and Halliwell-Phillipps. If these open-eyed German critics see more in the primrose than the littleness and inferiority of it, so do they also see more in the dramatic delineation of the character of Richard III. than the second-rate genius of a Marlowe, a Peele, or a Greene.

Schiller, with a true anti-Primrose spirit, closed his reading of 'Richard III.' with the splendid encomium: "It is one of the sublimest tragedies I know." Ulrici finds in 'Richard III.' the fifth act of the great tragedy of which 'Richard II.' is the first. In a very un-Primrose fashion, this philosopher makes bold to say: —

"No drama shows more distinctly than Henry VI. and its continuation Richard III. how the two sides of tragedy and comedy — according to their ethical significance — meet in the historical drama, and become blended into a higher unity."

Schlegel advances a similar theory, and implies the Shakespearian authorship of 'Richard III.' when he says: —

"These four plays ['Henry VI.' and 'Richard III.'] were undoubtedly composed in succession, as is proved by the style and the spirit in the handling of the subject: the last is definitely announced in the one which precedes it, and is also full of references to it; the same views run through the series; in a word, the whole make together only one single work."

This distinguished scholar thinks that the Englishmen's great admiration of this tragedy "is certainly in every respect well founded."

Dr. Gervinus, in his 'Shakespeare Commentaries,' unconsciously arrays himself against all Primrose Criticism when he bluntly and confidently says, with the assurance of a scholar : —

"Richard III. is Shakespeare's first tragedy of undoubted personal authorship; it is written in connection with Henry VI., and appears as its direct continuation."

But the great Professor comes into still closer collision with the Primrose Criticism when he says : —

"Richard III. shows extraordinary progress when compared to Henry VI. . . . The poetic diction, however much it reminds us of Henry VI., has gained surprisingly in finish, richness, and truth ; we need only compare the words of Anne at the beginning (Act I. Sc. 2) with the best parts of Henry VI., to find how thoroughly they are animated with the breath of passion, how pure and natural is their flow, and how entirely the expression is but the echo of the feeling."

It would seem that Primrose Criticism had involved itself in a vastly greater iconoclastic enterprise than it had bargained for, in its attempt to disprove the Shakespearian authorship of 'Richard III.,' since scientific criticism demands that the genuineness of all these related historical plays be invalidated together, or that they all stand together in their unquestioned integrity.

Attention is further called to the reasons laid down by the Primrose Criticism for robbing Shakespeare of his 'Richard III.'

It is asserted that the tragedy is not written in Shakespeare's style; that it proceeds with a different gait; that it contains nonsense and defective metre; that it is devoid of humor and eloquence; and that it contains whole scenes where the author's mind seems at dead low-tide throughout, and lays bare all its shallows and its ooze. With these serious charges made against the tragedy, singularly enough, not a shadow of a proof, not even an illustration or a quotation, is given in support of the charges.

It may again be suggested that it is remarkable that men of the poetical tastes of Jonson, Milton, Dryden, Pope, Schiller and Goethe; and men of the critical acuteness and ripe scholarship of Johnson, Steevens, Malone, Hazlitt, Lamb, Halliwell-Phillipps, and Richard Grant White; and men of the splendid histrionic genius of Burbage, Garrick, Cooke, Kean, Kemble, and Macready, have not detected the un-Shakespearian style, the alien, unknown, and vulgar gait of this remarkable 'Richard III.'

As to the "nonsense," it would be un-Shakespearian if it were absolutely free from it. The same is true of the "defective metre." If Sophocles, Æschylus, Corneille, Racine, or Voltaire were to be our model, then Shakespeare would be full of "nonsense." The violation or utter ignoring of the Unities, the trampling under foot of Aristotelian rules of dramatic composition, would be considered "nonsense" by the classical school. But if this be the "nonsense" for which 'Richard III.' is condemned, then must many a play of Shakespeare's come under the ban of condemnation. Nor is this the only kind of "nonsense" that may be found in Shakespeare's plays. Ben Jonson made this charge in his day : —

"His wit was in his owne power; would the rule of it had beene so too. Many times hee fell into those things, could not escape laughter: As when hee said in the person of *Cæsar*, one speaking to him: '*Cæsar thou dost me wrong.*' Hee replyed: '*Cæsar did never wrong, but with just cause:*' and such like; which were ridiculous. But he redeemed his vices, with his vertues."

Anachronisms are "nonsense" to those who measure by the classical standards; but if such "nonsense" is un-Shakespearian, — and none would seem greater to Aristotle, Ben Jonson, or Voltaire, — then must nearly every play of Shakespeare's be denied its accredited merit and high origin.

'Coriolanus' is marred and disfigured by the "nonsense" of Titus Lartius quoting Cato's estimate of a true soldier, when Cato was not born until two hundred and fifty years after the time in which Lartius mentions him. In the same play Menenius Agrippa refers to Alexander the Great, more than two hundred years before the conqueror of the world was born. And the same person speaks of "the most sovereign prescription in Galen," six hundred and fifty years before the great physician saw the light of day.

In the tragedy of 'Hamlet' we are astonished to hear Hamlet and the King in the tenth or eleventh century speak of the school at Wittenberg, which was not founded until 1502. Then reference is therein made to a performance of the play of 'Julius Cæsar,' which took place at the Oxford University in 1582! Several references are made to "brazen cannon" which were not in existence in Hamlet's time. Here is "nonsense"!

In 'Merry Wives of Windsor,' one may be surfeited with "nonsense." What right has Bardolph, in 1400, to know anything about "three German devils, three Doctor Faustuses"? What sense is there in Shallow's threatening Falstaff with, " I will make a Star-Chamber matter of it," when the Star-Chamber Court was not in existence? Mill sixpences were first coined in 1561, and the "Edward shovel-boards" not earlier than about 1550; yet Slender accuses Pistol, in 1400, of picking his pocket and robbing him "of seven groats of mill sixpences, and two Edward shovel-boards." Mrs. Ford, in a most unaccountable fashion, seemed to be familiar with the tune of "Green Sleeves" one hundred and seventy-five years before it was composed, which was in 1580. And Mr. Page had heard that "the Frenchman hath good skill in his rapier," nearly two hundred years before the rapier was introduced.

In the 'Winter's Tale' is the famous "nonsense" which provoked the ridicule of Ben Jonson, to which Drummond refers : —

"He said that Shakespeare wanted art, and sometimes sense; for in one of his plays he brought in a number of men, saying they had suffered shipwreck in Bohemia, where is no sea near by 100 miles."

To any sense but Primrose-sense it seems "nonsense" for one to put into a drama such a dialogue as this:—

"*Ant.* Thou art perfect then, our ship hath touch'd upon
The deserts of Bohemia?
    Mar.   Ay, my lord."

In 'Henry VI.' mention is made of Machiavel, who was but two years old when Henry VI. died.

It has been charged that it is "nonsense" for the dramatist to represent Fortinbras, in the tragedy of 'Hamlet,' as appearing at a certain time in Denmark, and in an hour and a half returning victorious from Poland. And it is equal "nonsense" to represent Othello as passing from Venice to Cyprus in a few moments of time.

All that Bowdler eliminated from the text of Shakespeare — "those words and expressions ... which cannot with Propriety be read aloud in a Family" — must be branded as "nonsense." The mixing up of tragedy and comedy in the same play is, by some, considered "nonsense." It would indeed be difficult to mention a species of "nonsense" that may not be found in Shakespeare. But there is hardly one of his plays that has less "nonsense" in it than 'Richard III.' This is true, whether the "nonsense" be the "nonsense" of vulgarity, of historical inaccuracy, of unnaturalness, or of the violation of the Unities of time and place. And the very criticism which would on the Primrose basis rob Shakespeare of 'Richard III.' would rob him of nearly every one of his great creations.

It may be of interest to take at least a glance at the suggestion that Shakespeare was so perfect in his poetic art that he could not have written in faulty style, nor in violation of any poetical canon. It is well known that he was admired by his contemporaries and immediate successors as a natural genius rather than as a trained and scholarly artist.

Ben Jonson, who knew Shakespeare personally, was candid in saying: "Shakespeare wanted Art. . . . His wit was in his owne power; would the rule of it had been so too."

Good Thomas Fuller expressed the common sentiment of the seventeenth century when he wrote of Shakespeare:—

"He was an eminent instance of the truth of that rule, '*Poeta non fit, sed nascitur;*' one is not *made*, but born a poet. Indeed his learning was very little, so that, as *Cornish diamonds* are not polished by any Lapidary, but are pointed and smoothed even as they are taken out of the earth, so *Nature* itself was all the *Art* which was used upon him."

Berkenhead, in praising Beaumont and Fletcher, most justly said : —

" Brave Shakespeare flow'd, yet had his Ebbings too,
Often above Himselfe, sometimes below."

Milton, master of poetic art, with taste and instinct exquisite, implies Shakespeare's deficiency in art as he listens to

"sweetest Shakespeare, Fancy's child,
Warble his native wood-notes wild."

Dryden honestly says of his idol : —

" I cannot say he is everywhere alike; were he so, I should do him injury to compare him with the greatest of mankind. He is many times flat, insipid; his comic wit degenerating into clinches, his serious swelling into bombast."

As compared with Jonson, this is Dryden's estimate of Shakespeare : —

" The *faultless* Johnson *equally* writ well;
Shakespeare made *faults*, but then did more excel."

Again this noble writer says : —

"Shakespeare, who many times has written better than any poet, in any language, is yet so far from writing wit *always*, or expressing that wit according to the dignity of the subject, that he writes, in many places, below the dullest writer of ours, or any precedent age."

Edward Phillips, the nephew of Milton, in his 'Theatrum Poetarum,' 1675, says:—

"Shakespeare, in spight of all his unfiled expressions, his rambling and indigested fancys, the laughter of the Critical, yet must be confessed a *poet* above many that go beyond him in Literature some degree."

And again:—

"From an Actor of Tragedies and Comedies he became a *Maker;* and such a *Maker*, that though some others may perhaps pretend to a more exact *Decorum* and *œconomie*, especially in Tragedy, never any express'd a more lofty and tragic height; never any represented nature more purely to the life, and where the polishments of Art are most wanting, as probably his Learning was not extraordinary, he pleaseth with a certain *wild* and *native* Elegance."

Pope, with most excellent judgment, wrote in his preface:—

"It must be owned, that with all these great excellencies, he has almost as great defects;

and that as he has certainly written better, so he has perhaps written worse, than any other."

Samuel Johnson made bold to ascribe certain faults to Shakespeare, by saying : —

"The style of Shakespeare was in itself ungrammatical, perplexed and obscure."

The criticisms quoted above apply to the nonsense, the faulty style, the defective metre, and the occasional commonplace passages to be found in Shakespeare's works.

From these criticisms the conclusion is to be drawn that, contrary to the opinion of the Primrose Criticism, Shakespeare wrote nonsense and indulged in defective metre. And this further conclusion is logical, that to reject the Shakespearian authorship of 'Richard III.' on the ground that it contains nonsense and defective metre, would warrant the rejection of nearly every play ascribed to Shakespeare. The faults of 'Richard III.' are not un-Shakespearian. And, with Professor Richardson, all may admit that "this tragedy, *like every work* of Shakespeare, has many faults."

It is further implied in the Primrose Criticism that as 'Richard III.' is without humor it lacks one of the infallible characteristics of

Shakespearian method and genius. Perhaps no play of this original dramatist adheres more closely to the classical standard with regard to its tragical unity than 'Richard III.' It lacks, let it be admitted, the unclassical admixture of comedy. But the play is of such an intensely cruel and tragic nature that it could with less consistency than any other play admit of the introduction of a comic strain. Its very diabolism seems to forbid any relief to the horror, or the admission of any ray of jest or clownishness into the damnable darkness. If, however, by the term "humor" we may include the idea of wit, sarcasm, cunning and adroit play of words, then, certainly, one of the greatest, if grimmest, humorists of Shakespeare's creation is Richard III. There are lines in the first soliloquy that contain humor. Gloster's wooing of Lady Anne, even in the presence of the corpse of Henry VI., is not only most eloquent, but consummately witty, bordering at least on the humorous. The strawberry subterfuge by which the Bishop of Ely is politely invited out of the council in the Tower, is a cheerful incident, if nothing more.

Nevertheless, it is true that this picture is very sparingly relieved of its sombre character by the comical or even by the humorous.

This fact, however, cannot rob the tragedy of its Shakespearian character, which is determined by its positive rather than by its negative elements, by what it contains rather than by what it lacks. A few of the great actors have so studied this play as to find in it rays of light, and in their acting they have relieved the play of the monotonous horror by bringing out the wit and even humor which they found therein. Kemble, Cooke, and Kean in particular were credited with the ability to find and to set forth these features of the dark tragedy. It was with difficulty that they succeeded.

On what grounds the Primrose Criticism insinuates that 'Richard III.' reveals a lack of patriotism in its author it is difficult to determine. If to portray reckless, heartless, insatiable ambition, a love of power which tramples underfoot the laws of God and society, — if to hold up to the universal gaze for everlasting execration

"That foul defacer of God's handy-work;
That excellent grand tyrant of the earth," —

if to record with dramatic force the diabolical intrigues, and the final, just calamities and ruin of a royal assassin and red-handed usurper, — be unpatriotic, then Shakespeare has indeed most successfully and commendably proven himself of an unpatriotic spirit. If patriotism means simply loyalty to a " House " or an administration rather than to the country, then of that narrow sort of patriotism Shakespeare, the author of ' Richard III.,' was not largely and conspicuously possessed. But that great tragedy was written by a pen which had been inspired with the loftiest patriotism, — a love of country and the rights of men. The spirit that wrote the play breathes in the patriotic prayer of Richmond : —

" O, now, let Richmond and Elizabeth,
　The true succeeders of each royal house,
　By God's fair ordinance conjoin together !
　And let their heirs (God, if thy will be so)
　Enrich the time to come with smooth-faced peace,
　With smiling plenty, and fair prosperous days !
　Abate the edge of traitors, gracious Lord,
　That would reduce these bloody days again,
　And make poor England weep in streams of blood !
　Let them not live to taste this land's increase,
　That would with treason wound this fair land's
　　peace !
　Now civil wounds are stopp'd, peace lives again ;
　That she may long live here, God say — Amen ! "

Primrose Criticism insinuates that to admit the Shakespearian authorship of this play would be to accuse the poet of therein permitting his mind to remain " at dead low-tide, and lay bare all its shallows and its ooze." It is difficult for one to understand Schiller's admiration of such a shallow and oozy-minded tragedy. And if these lines are at a poetic and dramatic "dead low-tide," what was "Marlowe's mighty line," when such a scholarly critic as Chalmers, in turning from Marlowe's play, must say:—

"Certain it is that when we open Shakespeare's Richard III. we seem to mount from the uniform flat, wherein we had been travelling with uncheered steps, to an exalted eminence, from whence we behold around us, an extensive country, diversified by hill and dale, refreshed by many waters, and traversed by roads, leading to hospitable mansions:

' *Glos.* Now is the winter of our discontent
Made glorious summer by this sun of York.' "

No "low-tide" performance here, to the mind of the Scotch antiquarian and critic!

All men have not been able to detect the shallows and ooze which the Primrose Criticism seems to find in 'Richard III.' Hazlitt had certainly seen virtues in this tragedy which escaped the eye of Peter Bell, for he wrote:—

"The play itself is undoubtedly a very powerful effusion of Shakespeare's genius. The groundwork of the character of Richard — that mixture of intellectual vigour with moral depravity, in which Shakespeare delighted to show his strength — gave full scope as well as temptation to the exercise of his imagination."

Coleridge must have found great excellences in this play; and his keen, critical eye must have overlooked the "shallows" and "ooze," else he could not have written: —

"Shakespeare here, as in all his great parts, develops in a tone of sublime morality the dreadful consequences of placing the moral in subordination to the mere intellectual being."

Let it not be supposed that an attempt is here made to prove the superiority of 'Richard III.' to all other Shakespearian productions. As a literary work it cannot hold rank with 'Hamlet,' 'Othello,' 'Lear,' and many other plays of this poet. Some may even wonder, with Johnson, Steevens, and Malone, why it has been so universally admired, without doubting its Shakespearian origin.

Hazlitt pronounces 'Richard III.' a play for the stage rather than for the study. Others criticise it for its inadaptability to the stage. Possibly the Cibber adaptation of the play was better calculated to produce theatrical effect than the original, but there can be no question that the 'Richard III.' of Shakespeare is the more perfect and admirable in the study. Indeed, the Cibber adaptation eliminates portions which, in the study and from the literary standpoint, are the finest portions of the play, and rank with the noblest and most elegant poetic strains of Shakespeare.

That which would be "dead low-tide," "shallows," "ooze," to the play-goer and to the actor, might be high-tide, ocean deeps, crystalline purity of philosophic thought and poetic form to the student and moralist.

Let it be admitted that some of the scenes and dialogues would be tedious and devoid of good taste and exciting interest on the stage; the same admission must be made touching many of Shakespeare's plays. If this fault is un-Shakespearian, surely there is hardly a purely Shakespearian play in existence. There are entire plays of Shakespeare which have never been popular on the stage, and quite a large number of them have entirely disappeared from the repertoire of the Shakespearian actors. Who of this generation has witnessed a successful and popular performance of 'Timon of Athens,' 'Pericles,' 'Titus Andronicus,' 'Cymbeline,' 'King John,' 'Henry VI.,' 'Troilus and Cressida,' 'Measure for Measure'?

But the drama is not to be judged and fashioned by the tastes and demands of the theatre alone. Doubtless many have agreed with Charles Lamb that Shakespeare cannot be acted, that the stage is not great enough for his dramatic creations. The theatre demanded that the original tragedy of 'Richard III.' should be changed; the change was made, and the play thereby gained popularity for the time being on the stage, but lost popularity in the study.

Colley Cibber almost destroyed the literary identity of the great tragedy when in 1700 he adapted it to the stage; yet he made the character of Richard, whose horrible identity he preserved, a great favorite with actors and play-goers. And though Garrick, Cooke, and Kean achieved fame in the performance of this mutilated play, who will say that Shakespeare, in *revisiting* "the glimpses of the moon," would be willing to adopt the "adaptation" and applaud Cibber for his pains? Who will acknowledge from the standpoint of literary dramatic criticism that the Cibber adaptation is equal to the original drama?

Now the argument is this, that a dramatic composition may be of high excellence from a literary and intellectual standpoint which on the stage, from an actor's or the auditor's point, would prove too intricate, obscure, tame, or even revolting. Such a play, however, does not necessarily reveal the "shallows" and "ooze" and "dead low-tide" of its author's mind; it may show the greater heights, depths, powers, and splendors of it.

Astonishment increases when this new Primrose Criticism makes the remarkable discovery that 'Richard III." is devoid of eloquence, and is not therefore of Shakespearian origin. It must be a very uncommon taste that is deaf to the eloquence of Richard's soliloquies, of Clarence's dream, of Margaret's curses, of Richmond's orations and prayers. Did not Gloster woo Lady Anne most eloquently? What can exceed the beauty and pathos of Edward's eulogy of his brother?

"*K. Edw.* Have I a tongue to doom my brother's death,
And shall that tongue give pardon to a slave?
My brother kill'd no man, his fault was thought,
And yet his punishment was bitter death.
Who sued to me for him? who, in my wrath,
Kneel'd at my feet, and bade me be advis'd?

Who spoke of brotherhood? who spoke of love?
Who told me, how the poor soul did forsake
The mighty Warwick, and did fight for me?
Who told me, in the field at Tewksbury,
When Oxford had me down, he rescu'd me,
And said, *Dear brother, live, and be a king?*
Who told me, when we both lay in the field,
Frozen almost to death, how he did lap me
Even in his garments; and did give himself,
All thin and naked, to the numb-cold night?
All this from my remembrance brutish wrath
Sinfully pluck'd, and not a man of you
Had so much grace to put it in my mind.
But when your carters or your waiting-vassals
Have done a drunken slaughter, and defac'd
The precious image of our dear Redeemer,
You straight are on your knees for pardon, pardon;
And I, unjustly too, must grant it you:—
But for my brother, not a man would speak,—
Nor I (ungracious) speak unto myself
For him, poor soul.— The proudest of you all
Have been beholden to him in his life;
Yet none of you would once plead for his life.—
O God! I fear, thy justice will take hold
On me, and you, and mine, and yours, for this.—
Come, Hastings, help me to my closet. O, poor
 Clarence!"

Is such an eloquence unworthy of Shakespeare's pen?

In reading Queen Elizabeth's farewell to the Tower which holds "those tender babes," and in reading Tyrrel's description of the "ruthless butchery," one joins with Hazlitt in pronouncing them "some of those wonderful bursts of feeling, done to the life, to the very height of fancy and nature, which our Shakespeare alone could give."

Has ever an actor in the noble character of Richmond doubted that he was pronouncing an eloquence equal to that of Henry V. before Harfleur, when on famous Bosworth field he harangued his troops, closing with the spirited and thrilling words : —

"Then, in the name of God, and all these rights,
Advance your standards, draw your willing swords :
For me, the ransom of my bold attempt
Shall be this cold corpse on the earth's cold face;
But if I thrive, the gain of my attempt
The least of you shall share his part thereof.
Sound, drums and trumpets, boldly and cheerfully;
God, and Saint George! Richmond, and victory!"

Not only the actions, but the very words of Richard on that fatal field were eloquent : —

"Fight, gentlemen of England! fight, bold yeomen!
Draw, archers, draw your arrows to the head!
Spur your proud horses hard, and ride in blood;
Amaze the welkin with your broken staves!"

"A thousand hearts are great within my bosom :
Advance our standards, set upon our foes;
Our ancient word of courage, fair Saint George,
Inspire us with the spleen of fiery dragons!
Upon them! Victory sits on our helms."

As Garrick acted the part, throwing into it the highest spirit of gallantry, what stirring eloquence was Richard's in the scene : —

> "*K. Rich.* A horse ! a horse ! my kingdom for a horse !
> *Catesby.* Withdraw, my lord, I 'll help you to a horse.
> *K. Rich.* Slave, I have set my life upon a cast,
> And I will stand the hazard of the die;
> I think, there be six Richmonds in the field;
> Five have I slain to-day, instead of him : —
> A horse ! a horse ! my kingdom for a horse !"

If eloquence be the test, 'Richard III.' is Shakespeare's.

The Primrose Criticism cannot suppress its mirth at the appearance of the ghosts on Bosworth field, and intimates that the scene is unworthy of Shakespeare, and hence was not his creation. Why Peter Bell does not laugh at the whole tribe of dramatic ghosts and every other sort of ghosts, is not apparent.

The ghosts in 'Hamlet,' 'Macbeth,' and 'Julius Cæsar' are as open to criticism, and are as provocative of mirth as the ghosts in 'Richard III.' Why Banquo's ghost should appear to Macbeth, and the ghost of the Royal Dane to Hamlet, and the ghost of Cæsar to Brutus, without challenging the criticism of Peter Bell, while the appearance of the ghosts of Richard's victims on Bosworth field should be thought laughable, is perhaps unworthy of serious inquiry. Whether any ghost scene be pleasing or not to the reader of this age, there is a seriousness of mind in which to study the dramatic requirements and necessities of an earlier age, which the Primrose Criticism does not seem to cultivate. There is at least a philosophical dignity, which should ever accompany criticism, to be found in Schlegel's remarks on the ghost scene in 'Richard III.' In explanation of Richard's heroic death, he says : —

"He fights at last against Richmond like a desperado, and dies the honorable death of a hero on the field of battle. Shakespeare could not change this historical issue, and yet it is by no means satisfactory to our moral feelings, as Lessing, when speaking of a German play on the same subject, has very judiciously remarked. How has Shakespeare solved this difficulty? By a wonderful invention he opens a prospect into the other world, and shows us Richard in his last moments already branded with the stamp of reprobation. We see Richard and Richmond in the night before the battle sleeping in their tents: the spirits of the murdered victims of the tyrant ascend in succession, and pour out their curses against him, and their blessings on his adversary. These apparitions are properly but the dreams of the two generals represented visibly. It is no doubt contrary to probability that their tents should only be separated by so small a space; but Shakespeare could reckon on poetical spectators who were ready to take the breadth of the stage for the distance between two hostile camps, if for such indulgence they were to be recompensed by beauties of so sublime a nature as this series of spectres and Richard's awakening soliloquy. The catastrophe of Richard the Third is, in respect to the external event, very like that of Macbeth; we have only to compare the thorough difference of handling them to be convinced that Shakespeare has most accurately observed poetical justice in the genuine sense of the word, that is, as signifying the relation of an invisible blessing or curse which hangs over human sentiments and actions."

It is certainly refreshing to turn from the Primrose sneer to such a philosophical criticism as this, which, if it serve no other end, may suggest the value of German seriousness above much American flippancy.

But why should Shakespeare be ridiculed for dramatizing tradition and history? The subject matter of the ghost scene was not invented by Shakespeare. The dramatist could not eliminate that part of Richard's experience. The historians told it all before the poet adapted it to the stage. The horrible dreams, the appearance of ghosts and even devils to the tormented mind of Richard on the eve of battle, are in the records. Let the Primrose Criticism attempt to dramatize this experience less ludicrously; let it undertake to do it more grandly and impressively.

Any criticism that overlooks the principal character of a drama must be logically defective if not scientifically worthless, however charmingly and elegantly it may be presented. Where criticism contents itself with pointing out the mote that dances in the beam of light, the withered leaf that hangs on the branch of the oak, the broken feather that still clings to the pinion of the eagle, the stain on the sail of the noble ship, the spot on the face of the glorious sun, the justice of the method may be seriously questioned. One of the most remarkable exhibitions of criticism ever witnessed was the recent notable Primrose study of the play of 'Richard III.' with Richard left out. Defective metre; poverty of style; lack of eloquence, humor, and patriotism; superfluity of ghost;

intellectual "dead low-tide," "shallows," "ooze;" and deliberate nonsense, — were dwelt upon with elegance and subtlety of assertion; but what of the character Richard III.? Nothing, absolutely nothing! And yet there is no other play of Shakespearian authorship that is so completely concentrated in one character as this. There is no other character that has become popular for the stage in which all the interests of the tragedy in which it is cast centre so completely. The play of 'Richard III.' leaves stamped upon the imagination and memory but one impression — Richard.

In a study of Shakespeare's other tragedies we find, for instance, that Hamlet, Othello, and Macbeth severally share with one or two other characters the interest of the play in which they appear. But Richard is himself alone. He is the whole play. And as he would not share the honors of the kingdom with another, but tyrannically demanded all and all the power usurped; so will he not share the interest of a dramatic plot with another: the play is his, the stage is his, as the kingdom is his alone. "Richard is the soul, or rather the dæmon, of the whole tragedy." However defective the metre, however lame the style, however tame the dialogue in certain parts, however dreary and even revolting some of the events and scenes in this tragedy, there stands a character which no pen but Shakespeare's could have delineated.

The most characteristic quality of Shakespeare's plays is the wonderful, unparalleled delineation of character to be found in them. Shakespeare was pre-eminent in his power " to hold, as 'twere, the mirror up to nature; to show virtue her own feature, scorn her own image, and the very age and body of the time his form and pressure." It is not the metre of the tragedy of 'Hamlet' that distinguishes it, and secures the immortality of its popularity, but the delineation of the character of Hamlet. It is not the absence of "nonsense," but the character of Shylock, that keeps up the world's interest in the 'Merchant of Venice.' It is not the literary style of the play of 'King Lear' that has placed it above all other modern tragedies; that is accomplished by the character of Lear. Neither the "patriotism" nor the "humor" of 'Macbeth,' but the character of Macbeth himself, as therein set forth, makes the tragedy great in literature and on the stage. So is it with the tragedy of 'Richard III.;' it is great because therein the characterization of Richard is great. No dramatic person that Shakespeare's mighty pen ever drew is more worthy of his genius. No character has won greater fame and popularity on the stage. No character, with the possible exception of Lear, demands in its representation the exercise of greater histrionic genius. There have been but four great Richards on the English stage, and they are the acknowledged greatest geniuses of the stage. If another hand than Shakespeare's drew this wonderful character, then let not Greene, Marlowe, Jonson, or Fletcher share the fame of the "Bard of Avon," but let the unknown author and creator of 'Richard III.' be partner in the possession of the greatest fame in dramatic literature.

Are we certain that Swift wrote the 'Tale of a Tub,' and Scott 'The Antiquary,' because nobody else could do it? Then Shakespeare drew the dramatic character of Richard III. because nobody else could do it. Yes, "there is a gait that marks the mind as well as the body;" and if not in the metre nor the literary style, in the great, impressive, terrible character of Richard III. may be detected the infallible, unmistakable mental gait of Shakespeare. It is submitted whether the Shakespearian character of any play in question is not to be determined rather from a study of the persons than of the prosody of the play.

Primrose Criticism will condescendingly admit that Shakespeare may have adapted the play to the stage, "making additions sometimes longer, sometimes shorter." But let it be noticed that the true author of the original play is not mentioned. No attempt is made to prove that the play had an existence in literature before 1597, when Shakespeare published it. Primrose Criticism is not wanting in antiquarian knowledge; let it therefore mention for the world's information just the play, with its title, date of publication, author's name, and dramatic plan, which Shakespeare laid his cunning if not thievish hand upon, and appropriated to himself. Will Primrose Criticism claim that it was Marlowe's play? or "A Tragical Report of King Richard, a Ballad," published in 1586? If so, there is an opportunity for candid comparison and argument.

George Steevens tells us — what many an antiquarian well knows — that several dramas on the present subject had been written before Shakespeare attempted it. If Shakespeare's attempt was not a new, an original, and a genuine production, then, in the name of critical fairness, it is unjust to charge Shakespeare with literary theft until it has been proven who else did write the play, or that it had a previous existence.

With all the poems and plays on this subject before them, after careful study and comparison, no editor, commentator, antiquarian, or critic has been able to find the original play or poem which Primrose Criticism accuses Shakespeare of stealing, revamping, and publishing in his own name. Common sense and common fairness suggest that there never existed such a play or poem, and that, until it is produced, Shakespeare is entitled to the honor and glory of having been the author of 'Richard III.'

That Shakespeare made his honey from the flowers that were blooming about him; that he did not create the silk and gold which he wove into the rich tapestries of his fancy; that he hewed from existing quarries the blocks out of which he constructed his gorgeous dramatic palaces, will be admitted. Not a play of his unquestioned authorship exists that does not bear proofs of his indebtedness to poets, historians, romancists, and translators, of his own and of preceding times. It is well known that there were already in existence and in common circulation the stories, poems, and chronicles which inspired or suggested the plots of Shakespeare's greatest plays. The stories of 'Hamlet,' 'Merchant of Venice,' 'Romeo and Juliet,' 'King Lear,' 'Macbeth,' 'Othello,' etc., were not original with Shakespeare; they were only modified and dramatized by him. This is the work and mission of the dramatist. In such a sense the tragedy of 'Richard III.' was a dramatization of an historical time and person.

For the historical basis of this tragedy Shakespeare depended upon others. He did not evolve his historical plays from his internal consciousness. That he received suggestions from poets, novelists, and dramatists who had written upon the same subject, is as probable as that he obtained necessary information from sober and learned historians. But detecting Plutarch, Boccaccio, Sir Thomas More, Holinshed, Hall, Grafton, Painter, Florio, and other authors and translators, in the dramatic works of Shakespeare does not justify the insinuation that he was a plagiarist.

Nor will a scientific criticism attempt on such ground to base an argument for the un-Shakespearian character and style of 'Richard III.'

Having noticed what seem to be some of the defects of the Primrose Criticism in its discussion of the Shakespearian authorship of 'Richard III.' it may not be unprofitable for us to turn to a short study of the sources from which Shakespeare drew the subject-matter of his tragedy.

PART II.

THE HISTORICAL BASIS OF 'RICHARD III.'

"My villainy they have upon record."

THE HISTORICAL BASIS OF RICHARD III.

GOETHE placed Shakespeare before all other poets for power of invention and for variety and originality of characterization. Yet he knew that the dramatist seldom, if ever, invented the subject matter of his plays. The jealousy of Greene has not biassed the judgment of fair-minded critics in determining Shakespeare's merit for originality. The author of 'Groats-worth of Wit' assailed Shakespeare after this fashion:

"There is an upstart Crow, beautified with our feathers, that with his *Tygers heart wrapt in a Players hide*, supposes he is well able to bombast out a blanke verse as the best of you: and being an absolute *Johannes factotum* is in his owne conceit the onely Shake-scene in a countrie. O, that I might entreate your rare wits to be employed in more profitable courses: and let those Apes imitate your past excellence, and never more acquaint them with your admired inventions."

It would take more than a groat's worth of such wit to convince the world that the 'sweet Swan of Avon,' with borrowed or with stolen wings, made

> " . . . those flights upon the banks of Thames
> That so did take Eliza and our James."

Few have had the temerity to charge Shakespeare with aping the excellences of superior wits. It was not necessary for that

> "Soule of the Age"

to depend upon the invention or originality of any other genius of his time;

> "Nature her selfe was proud of his designs,
> And joy'd to weare the dressing of his lines!"

Though Shakespeare, in common with all great dramatic poets, has borrowed the foundation material of his plays from history, fable, classic lore, and romance, yet his power of invention and his originality of genius are not to be questioned. His invention is shown, not in the creation of the figures of his plays, but in the elevation and transformation of them into poetic and dramatic characters. This, to the philosophical mind of Ulrici, " is proof of greater force and intensity of genius, greater truth and depth of intellect, than if he had himself invented the subject matter of his dramas."

For the subject matter of the historical tragedy of 'Richard III.,' Shakespeare was indebted to several sources, — historical and poetical. The principal sources were Holinshed, Grafton, Hall, Sir Thomas More, Marlowe, 'The True Tragedy of Richard III.,' and the 'Mirour for Magistrates.' If, as Walpole claims, the Shakespearian 'Richard' is not true to historical facts, then the blame of it must lie at the door of the historian rather than of the dramatist. It is beyond question, that the world bases its conception of Richard's character on Shakespeare's play, and that the dramatist has done more than any other to prejudice the world's opinion to the theory of the unmitigated diabolism of this infamous tyrant and usurper. But it will be found that the historians approach Shakespeare in the darkness of their representations; they approach him as nearly as sober, dispassionate history may approach impassioned drama.

The physical deformities of Richard, on which the poet makes him frequently soliloquize, both in ' Henry VI.' and ' Richard III.,' are minutely described by the historians. Several of the obscure or seemingly trifling passages of the play are suggested by Holinshed and More, and they appear in the play in almost the identical language of the historians. In illustration of these points reference is now made to the corresponding passages and descriptions found in the play, and the historical authorities on which the drama is based.

In the first soliloquy of Richard occur the lines : —

"But I, — that am not shap'd for sportive tricks,
Nor made to court an amorous looking-glass;
I, that am rudely stamp'd, and want love's majesty,
To strut before a wanton ambling nymph;
I, that am curtail'd of this fair proportion,
Cheated of feature by dissembling nature,
Deform'd, unfinish'd, sent before my time
Into this breathing world, scarce half made up,
And that so lamely and unfashionable,
That dogs bark at me, as I halt by them ; —
Why I, in this weak piping time of peace,
Have no delight to pass away the time ;
Unless to spy my shadow in the sun,
And descant on mine own deformity."

After his wooing of Lady Anne he again refers to his bodily deformity: —

"And will she yet abase her eyes on me,
That cropp'd the golden prime of this sweet prince,
And made her widow to a woful bed?
On me, whose all not equals Edward's moiety?
On me, that halt, and am mis-shapen thus?"

Lady Anne refers to Richard's physical condition when she cries: —

"Blush, blush, thou lump of foul deformity."

Again, spitting upon him and wishing her spittle were poison, she says: —

"Never hung poison on a fouler toad.
Out of my sight! thou dost infect mine eyes."

Queen Margaret's bitter curse contained the words: —

"Thou elvish-mark'd, abortive, rooting hog!
Thou that wast seal'd in thy nativity
The slave of nature, and the son of hell!
Thou slander of thy mother's heavy womb!
Thou loathed issue of thy father's loins!
Thou rag of honour!"

Again she cries: —

"Sin, death, and hell, have set their marks on him."

In the third part of 'Henry VI.,' Gloster soliloquizes: —

> "Why, love forswore me in my mother's womb;
> And, for I should not deal in her soft laws,
> She did corrupt frail nature with some bribe
> To shrink mine arm up like a wither'd shrub;
> To make an envious mountain on my back,
> Where sits deformity to mock my body;
> To shape my legs of an unequal size;
> To disproportion me in every part,
> Like to a chaos, or an unlick'd bear-whelp,
> That carries no impression like the dam."

In the eyes of King Henry, Gloster was

" . . . . . an indigest deformed lump."

There seems to be no exaggeration of Richard's physical deformities in Shakespeare's descriptions. The historian gives him no better aspect than the dramatist. The 'History of King Richard the Third,' written by Master Thomas More about the year 1513, contains the following description of Richard, in comparing him with his brothers Edward and Clarence:—

"Richarde the third sonne, of whom we nowe entreate, was in witte and courage egall with either of them, in bodye and prowesse farre under them bothe, little of stature, ill fetured of limmes, croke backed, his left shoulder much higher than his right, hard favoured of visage."

Holinshed drew largely upon Sir Thomas More and Grafton for his material. Shakespeare obtained his information directly from Holinshed rather than from More or Grafton. From the second edition of Holinshed's Chronicles, published in 1586, the following description of Richard is transcribed:—

"As he was small and little of stature, so was he of bodie greatlie deformed; the one shoulder higher than the other; his face was small, but his countenance cruell, and such, that at the first aspect a man would judge it to savour and smell of malice, fraud, and deceit.

"When he stood musing, he would bite and chew busilie his nether lip; as who said that his fierce nature in his cruell bodie alwaies chafed, stirred and was ever unquiet."

So much for Shakespeare's historical accuracy in his description of Richard's physical defects.

When Shakespeare makes Richard say,—

"I am determined to prove a villain,"

and in 'Henry VI.' puts into his mouth the terrible self-imprecation,—

"Then since the heavens have shap'd my body so,
Let hell make crook'd my mind to answer it,"

then draws a picture of Richard which carries out his determination into blackest deeds of villany and most hellish crookedness of mind, there is justification for it all in the historic records.

Sir Thomas More represents Richard's moral nature to be as deformed as his physical : —

"He was malicious, wrathfull, envious, and from afore his birth ever forwarde. . . . Hee was close and secrete, a deepe dissimuler, lowlye of counteynaunce, arrogant of heart, outwardly coumpinable where he inwardly hated, not letting to kisse whome hee thoughte to kyll : dispitious and cruell, not for evill will alway, but after for ambicion, and either for the suretie or encrease of his estate. Frende and foo was muche what indifferent, where his advauntage grew, he spared no mans deathe, whose life withstoode his purpose."

Holinshed wrote in the same strain : —

"Now when his death was knowne, few lamented, and manie rejoiced. The proud bragging white bore (which was his badge) was violentlie rased and plucked downe from everie signe and place where it might be espied : so ill was his life, that men wished the memorie of him to be buried with his carren corps. He

HISTORICAL BASIS OF 'RICHARD III.'

reigned two yeers, two moneths and one daie (too long by six and twentie months, and foure and twentie houres in most mens opinions, to whome his name and presence was as sweet and delectable, as his dooings princelie and his person amiable). . . . The dagger which he ware, he would (when he studied) with his hand plucke up and downe in the sheath to the midst, never drawing it fullie out: he was of a readie, pregnant, and quicke wit, wilie to feine, and apt to dissemble: he had a proud mind, and an arrogant stomach, the which accompanied him even to his death, rather choosing to suffer the same by dint of sword, than being forsaken and left helplesse of his unfaithfull companions, to preserve by cowardlie flight such a fraile and uncertaine life, which by malice, sicknesse, or condigne punishment was like shortlie to come to confusion. Thus ended this prince his mortall life with infamie and dishonor, which never preferred fame or honestie before ambition, tyrannie and mischiefe."

In the above estimate of Richard's character, Holinshed has quoted freely from Grafton, an earlier chronicler.

It is singular that Malone should have been of the opinion that Shakespeare was not indebted to 'The Mirour for Magistrates' in the composition of this tragedy. He says: "The Legend of King Richard III., by

Francis Seagars, was printed in the first edition of The Mirrour for Magistrates, 1559, and in that of 1575 and 1587; but Shakespeare does not appear to be indebted to it. In a subsequent edition of that book printed in 1610 the old legend was omitted, and a new one inserted by Richard Niccols, who has very freely copied the play before us." A perusal of the edition of 'The Mirour for Magistrates' published in 1587, ten years before Shakespeare's play was published, will reveal almost as much material for a tragedy of 'Richard III.' as may be found in More, Grafton, or Holinshed. It is sufficient to quote from the table of contents to show how fully the reign of Richard III. is therein treated. The work contains poems under the following titles: —

"60. How King Henry the Sixt, a vertuous Prince, was after many other miseryes, cruelly murdered in the Tower of London, the 22. of May. Anno. 1471.

"61. How George Plantagenet, thyrd sonne of the Duke of Yorke, was by his brother King Edward wrongfully imprysoned, and by his brother Richard miserably murdered, the 11. of January. Anno 1478.

"64. How the Lord Hastings was betrayed by trusting too much to his evill Councellour

Catesby, and villanously murdered in the Towre of London, by Richard Duke of Glocester, the 13. of June. Anno 1483.

"66. The complaynt of Henry Stafford, Duke of Buckingham.

"67. How Collingbourne was cruelly executed for making a foolish rime.

"68. How Richard Plantagenet Duke of Glocester, murdered his brothers children, usurping the Crowne : and in the 3. yeare of his raigne, was most worthely deprived of life and Kingdome in Basworth plaine, by Henry Earle of Richmond, after called King Henry the Seaventh: the 22. of August. 1485.

"73. How Shores wife, King Edward the fourths concubine, was by King Richard despoyled of all her goods, and forced to doe open penaunce."

Here would seem to be a rich field of resources for the dramatist, as all the persons figuring in the poems mentioned above are to be found in Shakespeare's tragedy of 'Richard III.'

In these poems the same character is given to Richard that may be found in More, Grafton, Holinshead, and Shakespeare.

In the poem on Lord Rivers occur the lines : —

"The Duke of Glocester that incarnate devill
Confedred with the Duke of Buckingham,

With eke Lord Hastings, hasty both to evill
To meete the King in mourning habit came,
(A cruell Wolfe though clothed like a Lambe.)"

In the poem on 'The complaynt of Henry Stafford, Duke of Buckingham,' that conspirator is made to say:—

"For having rule and riches in our hand
Who durst gaynesay the thing that wee averd?
Will was wisedome, our lust for law did stand,
In sort so straunge, that who was not afeard,
When hee the sounde but of King Richard heard?
So hatefull waxt the hearing of his name,
That you may deeme the residue of the same.

. . . .

So cruell seemde this Richard third to mee,
That loe myselfe now loathde his cruelty."

The poem on 'Richard Plantagenet, Duke of Glocester,' is prefaced with the remark of the supposititious story-teller:—

"I have here King Richards tragedy.... For the better understanding whereof, imagine that you see him tormented with Dives in the deepe pit of Hell, and thence howling this which followeth.

'What heart so hard, but doth abhorre to heare
The rufull raigne of me the third Richard?'" etc.

The poem represents Richard as confessing his cruelties; acknowledging that he "right did not regard," that in him "trust turned to treason," and

"Desire of a Kingdom forgetteth all kindred."

He says : —

"For right through might I cruelly defaced."

His crimes, he admits, brought the curses of men and God upon him, —

"For which I was abhorred both of yong and olde,
But as the deede was odious in sight of God and man,
So shame and destruction in the end I wan."

At the close of the poem the reader of it is made to say : —

"When I had read this, we had much talke about it. For it was thought not vehement enough for so violent a man as King Richard had been."

In defending the uncertain and broken metre of the poem, the reader says : —

"It is not meete that so disorderly and unnaturall a man as King Richard was, should observe any metricall order in his talke : which notwithstanding in many places of his oration is very well kepte : it shall passe therefore even as it is though too good for so evill a person."

Thus, in all these old authors, the villanous, diabolical character of Richard is set forth with most vigorous language.

Shakespeare seems completely justified in painting his dramatic portrait with the darkest colors, and on the authority of the historians he holds, "as 't were, the mirrour up to nature."

History justifies the bitter warning of Queen Margaret: —

"O Buckingham, beware of yonder dog;
Look, when he fawns, he bites; and when he bites,
His venom tooth will rankle to the death:
Have not to do with him, beware of him;
Sin, death, and hell, have set their marks on him;
And all their ministers attend on him."

Richard's mother, the Duchess of York, was historically justified in heaping upon the head of her cruel son the following accusations: —

". . . . . . . thou know'st it well,
Thou cam'st on earth to make the earth my hell.
A grievous burden was thy birth to me;
Tetchy and wayward was thy infancy;
Thy school-days frightful, desperate, wild and furious;
Thy prime of manhood, daring, bold, and venturous;
Thy age confirm'd, proud, subtle, sly, and bloody,
More mild, but yet more harmful, kind in hatred:
What comfortable hour canst thou name,
That ever grac'd me in thy company?"

The very conscience of Richard, as Shakespeare represents it, accords with the verdict of history : —

"My conscience hath a thousand several tongues,
And every tongue brings in a several tale,
And every tale condemns me for a villain.
Perjury, perjury, in the high'st degree;
Murder, stern murder, in the dir'st degree;
All several sins, all us'd in each degree,
Throng to the bar, crying all,— Guilty! guilty!"

Richmond's estimate of Richard is that of history : —

"A bloody tyrant, and a homicide;
One rais'd in blood, and one in blood establish'd;
One that made means to come by what he hath,
And slaughter'd those that were the means to help him;
A base foul stone, made precious by the foil
Of England's chair, where he is falsely set;
One that hath ever been God's enemy."

It must appear conclusive that Shakespeare did not depart from history in depicting the character of Richard III., but that in the darkest, most diabolical aspect of it he was supported by truth and fact.

It is interesting to trace to their sources the obscure references and seemingly far-fetched incidents which appear quite frequently in Shakespeare's lines, and have an historical basis.

In Richard's first soliloquy reference is made to a certain prophecy: —

"And, if King Edward be as true and just,
As I am subtle, false, and treacherous,
This day should Clarence closely be mew'd up
About a prophecy, which says — that G
Of Edward's heirs the murderer shall be.
Dive, thoughts, down to my soul! here Clarence
    comes.

(*Enter* CLARENCE, *guarded, with* BRAKENBURY.)

Brother, good day: What means this armed guard,
That waits upon your grace?
   Clar.   His majesty,
Tendering my person's safety, hath appointed
This conduct to convey me to the Tower.
   Glos. Upon what cause?
   Clar.   Because my name is — George.
   Glos. Alack, my lord, that fault is none of yours;
He should, for that, commit your godfathers: —
O, belike, his majesty hath some intent,
That you shall be new christen'd in the Tower.
But what 's the matter, Clarence? may I know?
   Clar. Yea, Richard, when I know; for, I protest,
As yet I do not: But, as I can learn,
He hearkens after prophecies, and dreams;
And from the cross-row plucks the letter G,
And says — a wizard told him, that by G
His issue disinherited should be;
And, for my name of George begins with G,
It follows in his thought, that I am he.

HISTORICAL BASIS OF 'RICHARD III.'

These, as I learn, and such like toys as these,
Have mov'd his highness to commit me now."

In 'The Mirour for Magistrates' may be found these lines, put into the mouth of the Duke of Clarence: —

"For by his Queene two Princelyke sonnes he had,
Borne to be punisht for their parents synne:
Whose Fortunes balked made the father sad,
Such wofull haps were found to be therein:
Which to avouch, writ in a rotten skin
A prophesie was found, which sayd a G,
Of Edwards children should destruction bee.

"Mee to bee G, because my name was George
My brother thought, and therefore did mee hate,
But woe be to the wicked heads that forge
Such doubtfull dreames to breede unkinde debate:
For God, a Gleve, a Gibbet, Grate, or Gate,
A Gray, a Griffeth, or a Gregory,
As well as George are written with a G."

In the poem on Lord Rivers, in the same book, reference is made to this prophecy, but with a different interpretation.

"Sir Thomas Vaughan chafing cryed still:
This tyrant Glocester is the gracelesse G
That will his brothers children beastly kyll."

Holinshed mentions this prophecy in his 'Life of Edward IV.:' —

"Some have reported, that the cause of this noble mans death rose of a foolish prophesie, which was, that after K. Edward one should reigne, whose first letter of his name should be a G. Wherewith the king and queene were sore troubled, and began to conceive a greevous grudge against the duke and could not be in quiet till they had brought him to his end. And as the divell is woont to incumber the minds of men which delite in such divelish fantasies, they said afterward, that that prophesie lost not his effect, when after king Edward, Glocester usurped his kingdome."

In the remarkable dialogue of the wooing scene between Lady Anne and Gloster, pointing to the corpse of Henry VI., Anne cries:

"O, gentlemen, see, see! dead Henry's wounds
Open their congeal'd mouths, and bleed afresh!
Blush, blush, thou lump of foul deformity;
For 't is thy presence that exhales this blood
From cold and empty veins, where no blood dwells;
Thy deed, inhuman and unnatural,
Provokes this deluge most unnatural."

This incident in the drama is based not only on the superstition that it was supposed the wounds of the victim bled afresh at the approach of the murderer, but also upon this record found in Holinshed's Chronicle:—

"The dead corps on the Ascension even was conveied with billes and glaves pompouslie (if you will call that a funerall pompe) from the

Tower to the church of saint Paule, and there laid on a beire or coffen barefaced, the same in presence of the beholders did bleed; where it rested the space of one whole daie. From thence he was caried to the Black-friers, and bled there likewise : and on the next daie after, it was conveied in a boat, without priest or clerke, torch or taper, singing or saieng, unto the monasterie of Chertsie, distant from London fifteene miles, and there was it first buried."

In Act II. Scene 3, a citizen is made to cry, —

" Woe to that land that 's govern'd by a child ! "

Sir Thomas More records these words in the oration of the Duke of Buckingham in the "yeld hall in London." Buckingham is haranguing the people in the interest of Richard, and dwelling upon his merits for the high office which he seeks, —

" Which roume I warne you well is no childes office. And that the greate wise manne well perceived. When hee sayde: *Veh regno cujus rex puer est.* Woe is that Realme, that hathe a chylde to theyre Kynge."

Reference is here made to Ecclesiastes x. 16 : —

" Woe to thee, O land, when thy king is a child."

Shakespeare, however, must have found this thought in More's 'Life of Richard III.,' or in Holinshed, who has transcribed the same oration from More or Hall into his own 'Life of Edward V.'

At a council held in the Tower (Act III. Scene 4) there are present Buckingham, Stanley, Hastings, the Bishop of Ely, Catesby, Lovel, Gloster, and others. For some unknown reason Gloster sends the Bishop of Ely from the Council on a very singular errand in these words:—

"*Glos.* My lord of Ely, when I was last in Holborn,
I saw good strawberries in your garden there;
I do beseech you send for some of them.
 Ely. Marry, and will, my lord, with all my heart."

The Bishop retires, and after a short time re-enters with,—

"Where is my lord protector? I have sent for these strawberries."

There seems to be very little, if any, sense in this strawberry incident, yet it was not invented by Shakespeare. It occurs in More and Holinshed in the following language:—

"These lordes so syting togyther comoning of thys matter, the protectour came in among them, fyrst aboute IX. of the clock, saluting them curtesly, and excusying himself that he had ben from them so long, saieng merely that he had bene a slepe that day. And after a little talking with them, he sayd unto the Bishop of Elye : My lord, you have very good strawberies at your gardayne in Holberne, I require you let us have a messe of them. Gladly my lord quod he, woulde god I had some better thing as redy to your pleasure as that. And therwith in al the hast he sent hys servant for a messe of strawberies."

Gloster withdraws from the Council for about an hour and returns. As he re-enters the Council with Buckingham the following dialogue takes place : —

"*Glos.* I pray you all, tell me what they deserve,
That do conspire my death with devilish plots
Of damned witchcraft; and that have prevail'd
Upon my body with their hellish charms?
 Hast. The tender love I bear your grace, my lord,
Makes me most forward in this noble presence
To doom the offenders: Whosoe'er they be,
I say, my lord, they have deserved death.
 Glos. Then be your eyes the witness of their evil,
Look how I am bewitch'd; behold mine arm
Is like a blasted sapling, wither'd up:
And this is Edward's wife, that monstrous witch,
Consorted with that harlot, strumpet Shore,
That by their witchcraft thus have marked me.
 Hast. If they have done this deed, my noble lord, —
 Glos. If! Thou protector of this damned strumpet,
Talk'st thou to me of ifs ? — Thou art a traitor : —

Off with his head: — now, by Saint Paul I swear,
I will not dine until I see the same. —
Lovel, and Catesby, look, that it be done;
The rest that love me, rise, and follow me."

The original version of this incident as given by More, and transcribed into the Chronicles of Hall and Holinshed has been very closely followed by Shakespeare, as will appear by the following, taken from More's 'Life of Richard III. :' —

" The protectour sette the lordes fast in comoning, and therupon praying them to spare hym for a little while, departed thence. And sone after one hower betwene X. and XI. he returned into the chamber among them, al changed with a wonderful soure angrye countenaunce, knitting the browes, frowning and froting and knawing on hys lippes, and so sat him downe, in hys place: al the lordes much dismaied and sore merveiling of this maner of sodain chaunge, and what thing should him aile. Then when he had sitten still a while, thus he began : What were they worthy to have, that compasse and ymagine the distruccion of me, being so nere of blood unto the king and protectour of his riall person and his realme. At this question, al the lordes sat sore astonied, musyng much by whome thys question should be ment, of which every man wyst himselfe clere. Then the lord chamberlen, as he that for the love betwene them thoughte he might be boldest with him, aunswered and sayd, that thei wer worthy to bee punished as heighnous traitors whatsoever they were. And al the other affirmed the same. . . . Then said the protectour: ye shal al se in what wise that sorceres and that other witch of her counsel Shoris wife with their affynite, have by their sorcery and witchcraft wasted my body. And therwith he plucked up hys doublet sleve to his elbow upon his left arme, where he shewed a werish withered arme and small, as it was never other. And therupon every mannes mind sore misgave them, well perceiving that this matter was but a quarel. . . . Netheles the lorde Chamberlen aunswered and sayd: certainly my lorde if they have so heinously done, thei be worthy heinouse punishment. What quod the protectour thou servest me I wene with iffes and with andes, I tel the thei have so done, and that I will make good on thy body traitour. And therwith as in a great anger, he clapped his fist upon the borde a great rappe. At which token given, one cried treason without the chambre. . . . And anon the protectour sayd to the lorde Hastings: I arest the traitour. What me my Lorde quod he. Yea the traitour, quod the protectour. . . . Then were they al quickly bestowed in divers chambres, except the lorde Chamberlen, whom the protectour bade spede and shryve hym a pace, for by saynt Poule (quod he) I wil not to dinner til I se thy hed of."

In Act III. Scene 2, the following dialogue occurs: —

"*Hast.* Cannot thy master sleep these tedious
  nights?
Mess. So it should seem by that I have to say.
First, he commends him to your noble lordship.
  Hast. And then, —
  Mess. And then he sends you word, he dreamt
To-night the boar had rased off his helm."

In the fourth scene Hastings is made to say: —

" Woe, woe, for England! not a whit for me;
  For I, too fond, might have prevented this:
  Stanley did dream, the boar did rase his helm;
  But I disdain'd it, and did scorn to fly.
  Three times to-day my foot-cloth horse did stumble,
  And startled, when he look'd upon the Tower,
  As loath to bear me to the slaughter-house."

More and Holinshed are Shakespeare's authorities for the subject matter of the above-mentioned incidents.

More writes: —

"A marveilouse case is it to here, either the warnings of that he shoulde have voided, or the tokens of that he could not voide. For the self night next before his death, the lord Stanley sent a trustie secret messenger unto him at midnight in al the hast, requiring hym to rise and ryde away with hym, for he was disposed utterly no longer to bide : he had so fereful a dreme, in which him thoughte that a bore with his tuskes so raced them both bi the heddes, that the blood ranne aboute both their shoulders. And forasmuch as the protector gave the bore for his cognisaunce, this dreme made so fereful an impression in his hart, that he was thoroughly determined no longer to tary, but had his horse redy, if the lord Hastinges wold go with him to ride so far yet the same night, that thei shold be out of danger ere dai . . .

"Certain it is also, that in the riding toward the tower, the same morning in which he was behedded, his horse twise or thrise stumbled with him almost to the falling, which thing albeit eche man wote wel daily happeneth to them to whom no such mischaunce is toward: yet hath it ben of an olde rite and custome, observed as a token often times notably foregoing some great misfortune."

Holinshed follows More word for word in recording the above incidents.

Gloster urges Buckingham to appear before the people to shake their confidence in the legitimacy of Edward and Clarence (Act III. Scene 5) : —

"*Glos.* Go, after, after, cousin Buckingham.
The mayor towards Guildhall hies him in all post : —
There, at your meetest vantage of the time,
Infer the bastardy of Edward's children :
. . . . . .

> *Buck.* Doubt not my lord; I'll play the orator,
> As if the golden fee, for which I plead,
> Were for myself: and so, my lord, adieu.
>   *Glos.* If you thrive well, bring them to Baynard's castle;
> Where you shall find me well accompanied,
> With reverend fathers, and well-learned bishops."

They meet again in the court of Baynard's castle (Act III. Scene 7):—

> "*Glos.* How now, how now? What say the citizens?
>   *Buck.* Now by the holy mother of our Lord,
> The citizens are mum, say not a word.
>   *Glos.* Touch'd you the bastardy of Edward's children?
>   *Buck.* I did; . . .
> . . . .
> I bade them that did love their country's good,
> Cry — *God save Richard, England's royal king!*
>   *Glos.* And did they so?
>   *Buck.* No, so God help me, they spake not a word;
> But, like dumb statuas, or breathing stones,
> Star'd on each other, and look'd deadly pale.
> Which when I saw, I reprehended them;
> And ask'd the mayor, what meant this wilful silence;
> His answer was, — the people were not us'd
> To be spoke to, but by the recorder.
> Then he was urg'd to tell my tale again;—
> *Thus saith the duke, thus hath the duke inferred;*
> But nothing spoke in warrant from himself.
> When he had done, some followers of mine own,
> At lower end o' the hall, hurl'd up their caps,
> And some ten voices cried, *God save king Richard!*
> And thus I took the vantage of those few, —

> *Thanks, gentle citizens, and friends,* quoth I;
> *This general applause, and cheerful shout*
> *Argues your wisdom, and your love to Richard:*
> And even here brake off, and came away."

Sir Thomas More gives in full Buckingham's oration, which was historically spoken for the very purpose indicated by Shakespeare in the drama. More has also left on record the effect of the oration on the people:—

"When the duke had saied, and looked that the people whome he hoped that the Mayor had framed before, shoulde after this proposicion made, have cried, king Richarde, king Richarde: all was husht and mute, and not one word aunswered thereunto. . . . And by and by somewhat louder, he rehersed them the same matter againe in other order and other wordes. . . . But were it for wonder or feare, or that eche looked that other shoulde speake fyrste: not one woorde was there aunswered of all the people that stode before, but al was as styl as the midnight, . . . when the Mayor saw thys he wyth other pertners of that counsayle, drew aboute the duke and sayed that the people had not ben accustomed there to be spoken unto but by the recorder. . . . At these wordes the people began to whisper among themselves secretly, that the voyce was neyther loude nor distincke, but as it were the sounde of a swarme of bees, tyl at the last in the nether ende of the hal, a bushement of the dukes servants and Nashefeldes and other longing to the protectour, with some prentises and laddes that thrust into the hal amonge the prese, began sodainely at mennes backes to crye owte as lowde as their throtes would gyve: king Richarde kinge Richarde, and threwe up their cappes in token of joye. And they that stode before, cast back theyr heddes mervaileling thereof, but nothing they sayd. And when the duke and the Maier saw thys maner, they wysely turned it to theyr purpose. And said it was a goodly cry and a joyfull to here, every man with one voice no manne sayeng nay."

In this matter Holinshed transcribes literally from Sir Thomas More.

When, in Act IV. Scene 2, Richard proposes to Buckingham to make way with Edward, the Duke hesitates, and asks for time to consider the matter. This angers Richard, who descended from his throne, gnawing his lip and muttering: —

"*K. Rich.* I will converse with iron-witted fools,
And unrespective boys; none are for me,
That look unto me with considerate eyes; —
High reaching Buckingham grows circumspect. —
Boy, ——
   Page. My lord.
   K. Rich. Know'st thou not any whom corrupting
      gold
Would tempt unto a close exploit of death?

HISTORICAL BASIS OF 'RICHARD III.' 93

Page. I know a discontented gentleman,
Whose humble means match not his haughty mind:
Gold were as good as twenty orators,
And will, no doubt, tempt him to anything.
K. Rich. What is his name?
Page. His name, my lord, is Tyrrel.
K. Rich. I partly know the man; Go, call him hither, boy."

The page brings Tyrrel into the presence of Richard, who engages him to make way with

". . . those bastards in the Tower."

This incident is based upon, but is a slight modification of, the historical record to be found in Holinshed and More. It appears that Richard sent one John Grene with a letter to Sir Robert Brakenbury, constable of the Tower, requesting him to put the princes to death. Brakenbury refused to commit the murder. Grene returned with the refusal to Richard, —

"wherwith he toke such displeasure and thought, that the same night, he said unto a secrete page of his: Ah whome shall a man trust? those that I have broughte up myselfe, those that I had went would most surely serve me, even those fayle me, and at my commanndemente wyll do nothyng for me. Sir quod his page there lyeth one on your paylet without, that I dare well say to do your grace pleasure, the thyng were right harde that he wold refuse, meaning this by sir James Tyrell, which was a man of right goodlye personage, and for natures gyftes, woorthy to have served a muche better prince, if he had well served god, and by grace obtayned as muche trouthe and good wil as he had strength and witte. . . . For upon this pages wordes king Richard arose, and came out into the pailet chamber, on which he found in bed sir James and sir Thomas Tyrels, of parson like and brethren of blood, but nothing of kin in condicion. Then said the king merely to them: What? sirs, be ye in bed so soone, and calling up syr James, brake to him secretely his mind in this mischievous matter. In whiche he founde him nothing strange," etc.

In Act IV. Scene 4, Margaret speaks of Richard as

"That dog, that had his teeth before his eyes,
To worry lambs, and lap their gentle blood."

And the Duchess of York, addressing Richard, says: —

"A grievous burden was thy birth to me."

In 'Henry VI.' the King addresses Gloster with the reproachful words: —

"Thy mother felt more than a mother's pain,
And yet brought forth less than a mother's hope;
. . . .

Teeth had'st thou in thy head, when thou wast born,
To signify, — thou cam'st to bite the world."

After stabbing the King, Gloster soliloquizes : —

"Indeed, 't is true, that Henry told me of;
For I have often heard my mother say,
I came into the world with my legs forward;
. . . . . .
The midwife wonder'd; and the women cried,
O, Jesus bless us, he is born with teeth !"

More and Holinshed give the historical basis for these incidents of the birth of Richard referred to in Shakespeare's drama : —

"It is for trouth reported, that the Duches his mother had so muche a doe in her travaile, that shee coulde not bee delivered of hym uncutte: and that hee came into the worlde with the feete forwarde, as menne bee borne outwarde, and (as the fame runneth) also not untothed."

In Act IV. Scene 4, Richard entreats Queen Elizabeth to plead his suit with her daughter.

"*K. Rich.* Then in plain terms tell her my loving tale.
Q. Eliz. Plain and not honest, is too harsh a style.
K. Rich. Your reasons are too shallow and too quick.

Q. Eliz. O, no, my reasons are too deep and dead;—
Too deep and dead, poor infants, in their graves.
K. Rich. Harp not on that string, madam; that is past.
Q. Eliz. Harp on it still shall I, till heart-strings break."

As the figure "Harp not on that string" occurs in More's 'Life of Richard III.,' it is reasonable to suppose, though it had long been a common expression, that Shakespeare borrowed it from More or from Holinshed, though he uses it in a different connection and puts it into the mouth of a different person.

The Lord Cardinal engages in a discussion with Queen Elizabeth on the use and abuse of sanctuary, in which Lord Howard joins. The latter by an indiscreet remark brings a mild rebuke upon himself. Sir Thomas More writes:—

"The Cardinall made a countinance to the other Lord, that he should harp no more upon that string."

In the histories these words are spoken in the presence of Elizabeth, but are addressed by the Cardinal to Lord Howard; in the drama they are addressed to Elizabeth by

Richard. It is very probable that Shakespeare found the suggestion in the history.

On the eve of the day of battle Richard, having made arrangements for the conflict, proceeds to his tent with, —

> "So, I am satisfied. Give me a bowl of wine:
> I have not that alacrity of spirit,
> Nor cheer of mind, that I was wont to have."

This corresponds with the historical record as found in Holinshed : —

> "His heart being almost damped, he prognosticated before the doubtfull chance of the battell to come; not using the alacritie and mirth of mind and countenance as he was accustomed to doo before he came toward the battell."

The ghost scenes and the troubled dreams of Richard on the eve of battle, so vividly represented by the masterly pen of Shakespeare, were not purely imaginary and created for dramatic effect; they were based on history or tradition, and belonged to the life and experience of Richard.

No less than eleven ghosts rise to predict disaster for Richard in the approaching battle ; they are the ghosts of his murdered victims, and their appearance fills him with terror. As they vanish he starts from his dream, with, —

"Give me another horse, — bind up my wounds, —
Have mercy, Jesu ! — Soft ; I did but dream.
O coward conscience, how dost thou afflict me !
The lights burn blue. — It is now dead midnight.
Cold fearful drops stand on my trembling flesh.
What do I fear ? Myself ? there's none else by :
Richard loves Richard ; that is, I am I.
Is there a murderer here ? No ; — Yes ; I am :
Then fly. — What, from myself ? Great reason :
    Why ?
Lest I revenge. What ? Myself on myself ?
Alack ! I love myself. Wherefore ? for any good,
That I myself have done unto myself ?
O, no : alas, I rather hate myself,
For hateful deeds committed by myself.
I am a villain : Yet I lie, I am not.
Fool, of thyself speak well : — Fool, do not flatter.
My conscience hath a thousand several tongues,
And every tongue brings in a several tale,
And every tale condemns me for a villain.
Perjury, perjury, in the high'st degree ;
Murder, stern murder, in the dir'st degree ;
All several sins, all us'd in each degree, —
Throng to the bar, crying all, — Guilty ! guilty !
I shall despair. — There is no creature loves me ;
And, if I die, no soul will pity me ; —
Nay, wherefore should they ? since that I myself
Find in myself no pity to myself.
Methought, the souls of all that I had murder'd
Came to my tent : and every one did threat
To-morrow's vengeance on the head of Richard."

On the morning of the fatal day, Ratcliff enters Richard's tent, when the trembling King says : —

"O Ratcliff, I have dream'd a fearful dream! —
What thinkest thou? Will our friends prove all true?
Rat. No doubt, my lord.
K. Rich.   Ratcliff, I fear, I fear, —
Rat. Nay, good my lord, be not afraid of shadows.
K. Rich. By the apostle Paul, shadows to-night
Have struck more terror to the soul of Richard,
Than can the substance of ten thousand soldiers,
Armed in proof, and led by shallow Richmond."

The historical basis for such dramatic representation as the above may be found in the following passages from More, Grafton, and Holinshed. More says : —

"I have heard by credible report of such as wer secrete with his chamberers, that after this abbominable deede done, he never hadde quiet in his minde, hee never thought himself sure. Where he went abrode, his eyen whirled about, his body privily fenced, his hand ever on his dager, his countenance and maner like one alway ready to strike againe, he toke ill rest a nightes, lay long wakyng and musing, sore weried with care and watch, rather slumbered than slept, troubled wyth fearful dreames, sodainly somme tyme sterte up, leape out of his bed and runne about the chamber, so was his restles herte continually tossed and tumbled with the tedious impression and stormy remembrance of his abominable dede."

Holinshed moralizes on the disturbed condition of Richard's mind : —

"Than the which there can be no greater torment. For a giltie conscience inwardlie accusing and bearing witnesse against an offendor, is such a plague and punishment, as hell itsclf (with all the feends therein) can not affoord one of greater horror and affliction."

In Grafton's Chronicles it is written : —

"In the meane season, Kyng Richarde . . . marched to a place meete for two battayles to encounter by a Village called Bosworth, not farre from Leycester, and there he pitched hys fielde, refreshed hys souldyours and toke his rest. The fame went that he had the same night a dreadfull and a terrible dreame, for it seemed to him beyng a sleepe that he sawe dyvers ymages like terrible Devils which pulled and haled him, not suffering him to take any quiet or rest. The which straunge vision not so sodainly strake his hart with a sodaine feare, but it stuffed his head and troubled his minde with many dreadfull and busie imaginations. . . . And least that it might be suspected that he was abashed for feare of his enemies, and for that cause looked so pitteously, he recyted and declared to his familiar friends in the morning his wonderful vision and terrible dreame. But I think this was no dreame, but a punction and prick of his sinnefull conscience, for the conscience is so much more charged and aggravate as the offence is greater and more heynous in degree."

Holinshed adds to Grafton's words his own moralizing: —

"So that king Richard, by this reckoning, must needs have a woonderfull troubled mind, because the deeds that he had doone, as they were heinous and unnaturall, so did they excite and stirre up extraordinarie motions of trouble and vexations in his conscience."

Now, if the Primrose Criticism would laugh when ghosts rise before the tent of Richard, let it laugh at Sir Thomas More, Grafton, Holinshed, tradition, and history; not at Shakespeare, who merely dramatized the incident.

The orations of Richard and Richmond on the field of battle Shakespeare has condensed from Grafton's and Holinshed's Chronicles, where they appear in full. The dramatist has preserved the ideas expressed, and, in many cases, the language and figures used by the historians. So closely do the speeches of Richard and Richmond, as they appear in Shakespeare, follow those found in

Holinshed, that they would be considered plagiarisms if put into the mouths of other persons.

In the historic oration Richard speaks of the "beggarly Britons" and "faynt harted Frenchmen" who come against them. In the play he calls them

> " A sort of vagabonds, rascals, and runaways,
> A scum of Bretagnes and base lackey peasants;"

and he cries: —

> " Let 's whip these stragglers o'er the seas again;
> Lash hence these over-weening rags of France;
> These famished beggars weary of their lives."

In speaking of Richmond, in the historic oration, he says: —

"And to begin with the erle of Richmond, capteine of this rebellion, he is a Welsh milkesop, a man of small courage, and of lesse experience in martiall acts and feats of warre, brought up by my moothers meanes and mine, like a captive in a close cage in the court of Franncis duke of Britagne; and never saw armie," etc. (Holinshed.)

In the dramatic oration Richard says: —

> " And who doth lead them, but a paltry fellow,
> Long kept in Bretagne at our mother's cost?

> A milk-sop, one that never in his life
> Felt so much cold as overshoes in snow?"

Richmond says, in his historic oration:—

"I doubt not but God wil rather aide us (ye and fight for us). . . . Our cause is so just that no enterprise can be of more vertue, both by the lawes divine and civile." (Grafton.)

In the play he says:—

"God, and our good cause, fight upon our side."

Again, the Chronicles put these words into Richmond's mouth:—

"What can be more honest, goodly, or godly quarrell than to fight against a Captayne, being an homicide, and a murderer of his owne blood, and progenie?
"Who will spare yonder tirant, Richard Duke of Glocester untruly calling himself king, considering that he hath violated, and broken both the lawe of God and man, what vertue is in him, which was the confusion of his brother, and murtherer of his Nephewes?"

In the play Richmond says:—

> "For what is he they follow? truly, gentlemen,
> A bloody tyrant, and a homicide;
> One rais'd in blood, and one in blood establish'd;
> One that made means to come by what he hath,

> And slaughter'd those that were the means to help him;
> A base foul stone, made precious by the foil
> Of England's chair, where he is falsely set;
> One that hath ever been God's enemy: " etc.

This interesting comparison of the speeches of the play with the speeches of the chronicle might be followed still further; but enough has been done to show that the drama does not vary from history in the substance of these battle harangues.

It is acknowledged that this short chapter cannot, even as a whole, claim to be an exhaustive comparison of the play of 'Richard III.' with the historical authorities on which it is based. There are many other incidents in the play the origin of which might easily be traced to tradition and history; but a sufficient number of illustrations have been produced to indicate beyond all question the true sources of the subject matter of 'Richard III.'

It may be found in several instances that Shakespeare has written nonsense, for which critics hold him responsible, when the nonsense is the result of the historian's mistakes or weaknesses. Historical accuracy is one of the merits of this tragedy of 'Richard III.,' "wherein," says Milton, "the Poet us'd not much Licence in departing from the truth of History, which delivers him a deep Dissembler, not of his affections only, but of Religion."

The Richard of Shakespeare is the Richard of History.

PART III.

THE HISTRIONIC RICHARDS.

"Suit the action to the word, the word to the action; with this special observance, that you o'erstep not the modesty of nature: for anything so overdone is from the purpose of playing, whose end, both at the first, and now, was, and is, to hold, as 't were, the mirrour up to nature: to show virtue her own feature, scorn her own image, and the very age and body of the time, his form and pressure."

THE HISTRIONIC RICHARDS.

THE stage is not the best interpreter of Shakespeare. It has been the most efficient corrupter of that supreme dramatist. The mutilations of the original text, the interpolations and eliminations, which have rendered it almost impossible to determine what Shakespeare originally wrote, have originated in the theatre. Very few of the actors of the English stage have been scholars, though many of them have ranked with men of highest native intellectuality and taste.

Many a genius has been able to catch the spirit of Shakespeare's characters, and to present upon the stage thrilling and captivating performances, who has lacked the knowledge, learning, critical acumen, and literary taste necessary to a thorough and scientific study of Shakespeare as a literature. It is well known that Kemble, Cooke, Kean, and J. B. Booth made some of their most telling "points" by glaring misinterpretations of Shakespeare's thought. It has not infrequently transpired that the actor has given to a Shakespearian character an interpretation which, while it stamped the performance with the actor's genius or eccentricity, almost destroyed its Shakespearian identity. The student and scholar of to-day owe more to Pope, Theobald, Hanmer, Johnson, Steevens, Malone, Ulrici, Goethe, Gervinus, Collier, Halliwell-Phillipps, and Richard Grant White, for present light on everything that is Shakespearian in literature, than to all the actors that have strutted the stage from the days of Burbage to the age of Salvini, Irving, and Edwin Booth. Actors have not enriched the theme by any valuable restorations to the text, any wise verbal criticism, any antiquarian research and discovery, any etymological or grammatical elucidations, any historical or classical illustrations of importance. For all these important helps to the study and comprehension of Shakespeare we are indebted to men of letters and of the academic gown rather than to men of the sock and buskin.

It is nevertheless interesting to consider the merits of those great actors who by common consent have been the finest interpreters of Shakespeare on the stage. In calling to our attention the greatest Richards of the theatre it is not surprising that we are compelled to summon before us the greatest actors, the most conspicuous histrionic geniuses that have graced the English stage. No mean actor has ever been able to worthily represent Richard III., which fact must add peculiar lustre to the fame of its author.

The first, the original Richard, was a friend and a fellow actor of Shakespeare, and doubtless studied the great character in the light of its author's instruction. This was Richard Burbage, "England's great Roscius." He was born in 1566, two years after the great poet, and died in 1619, surviving his illustrious friend but three years. The name of this renowned actor appears second in the list of Principal Actors, of which Shakespeare's is first, printed in the first folio edition of the poet's works. Reference has already been made to the Tooley anecdote, in which both Burbage and Shakespeare assume the name of Richard III. The story would indicate that Burbage was as universally recognized to be the actor of the character as Shakespeare was to be the author of it.

In a play performed at one of the Universities, while Burbage was performing this tragedy and making fame in the character of Richard, the actor is represented as teaching an apt pupil how to perform the part; which would also seem to intimate that he was recognized to be the Richard of his day, and the authority on the subject so far as the theatrical representation of the character was concerned. In the literature of his day, Burbage is perhaps more conspicuously and eulogistically identified with this than with any other character which he assumed. Bishop Corbet represents that when he visited Bosworth field his host confounded Burbage with Richard in describing the battle, showing what a profound impression the actor had made in this character.

"Besides what of his knowledge he could say,
He had authentic notice from the play,
Shown chiefly by that one perspicuous thing,
That he mistook a player for a King;
For when he should have said, here Richard died
And called 'a horse, a horse' — he Burbadge cried."

Burbage must have resembled Garrick in universality and versatility of genius, as he assumed all the most important Shakespearian characters with ability and success. In his death the theatrical, if not the literary world mourned the disappearance from the stage of all these great characters, — his "Young Hamlet, though but Scant of breath," "poor Romeo," "Tyrant Macbeth, with unwash'd bloody hand," "the red-hair'd Jew," "the grieved Moor," — and all his parts, "From ancient Leare to youthful Pericles;" but it was above all felt by that age that in Burbage's death,

"*The* Crookback, as befits, shall cease to live."

In stature, Burbage was short and thickset; his features were wonderfully expressive, as the lines of the elegy run : —

"Thy stature small, but every thought and mood
Might thoroughly from thy face be understood."

His every action was truth and grace, and his voice and elocution were enchanting.

"How did his speech become him, and his pace
Suit with his speech, and every action grace
Them both alike, while not a word did fall
Without just weight to ballast it withal.
Had'st thou but spoke with Death, and us'd the power
Of thy enchanting tongue at that first hour

Of his assault, he had let fall his dart
And quite been charm'd with thy all-charming art."

If the eulogies may be accepted, Burbage has had no superior on the stage, not even excepting Garrick or Kean. What, then, must have been that Richard, which was his greatest representation, and which he undoubtedly studied and performed with Shakespeare's assistance? No reliable traditions have come down to us of his "points" and peculiar excellences in this character. His creation — for he was beyond dispute the original Richard — seems to have perished with him. Crookback, as was fit, did cease to live. A hundred years passed by ere another rose to assume the almost forgotten character. Across those years no definite, intelligent ideas of Burbage's performance had come. The great Burbage and the great Richard, like the greater Shakespeare, passed away without leaving to the historian a satisfying portion, nor even to the curious more than a few dry crumbs of tradition.

Thomas Betterton was doubtless in some of his characters the equal if not the superior of Burbage. Pepys wrote: "I only know that Mr. Betterton is the best actor in the world," and of this actor's first soliloquy in 'Hamlet,' he exclaimed: "It's the best acted part ever done by man." Yet Betterton did not make any fame in the character of Richard. His corpulency and general ungainly and clumsy proportions unfitted him for this character, though his voice, not unlike Kean's and Cooke's in natural gruffness, might have been adapted to the part. The greatest Hamlet, however, was not even a tolerable Richard. Colley Cibber, who, in 1700, mutilated the play of 'Richard III.' to adapt it to the stage, attempted the leading role, but failed. Barton Booth, so distinguished in Addison's 'Cato,' could not master the energy and genius to produce

"That excellent grand tyrant of the earth."

Macklin, —

". . . . . the Jew
That Shakespeare drew,"

was unequal to the task of performing a great Richard.

The first actor to pick up the long-neglected mantle of Burbage and assume with originality and success the character of Richard III., was Lacy Ryan, who began to attract attention about the year 1712. This now almost forgotten actor was doubtless the creator of the Richard of the modern stage. To him Garrick, Cooke, Kean, and Booth were indebted for many of their "points." Foote was so impressed with Ryan's acting in this part that he wrote to his praise: —

"From him succeeding Richards took the cue,
And hence his style, if not the color, drew."

Fitzgerald, the biographer of Garrick, acknowledges the great actor's indebtedness to Ryan, and Garrick himself attributed the merits of his own representation to Ryan, whom he had gone to ridicule in the play of 'Richard III.,' but came away to admire, praise, and imitate.

Ryan's Richard must have received its excellences from his mental rather than from his physical advantages. If so, the greater the virtue and more just the praise. While Ryan's general features were favorable, his nose had been broken by a blow, and his cheeks pierced and jaw broken by a bullet. The result of these injuries was an irremediable defect of voice and elocution. He gave but little attention to his "make up," and often appeared in a part with slovenly dress, which, with a lack of natural grace and his absolute ignorance of gesture, detracted from the external merits of his representation. In spite of these disadvantages, however, he made an impression in the character of Richard III., which has come down, through the imitations of the greatest actors, to the present time. Lacy Ryan must have possessed an uncommon genius to have risen above all his physical defects into a character which is in many important features the stage Richard of to-day.

On Oct. 19, 1741, David Garrick made his debut at Goodman's Fields as Richard III. It was a wise choice of character, though one of the most trying parts that ever actor attempted. His debut was not only a success, but his performance of Richard was the sensation of the day. All London was in a furor of dramatic excitement; and the *élite* of the city thought it no task to drive out to Goodman's Fields to witness the great Shakespearian representation, while even the most distinguished congratulated themselves on their good fortune if they succeeded in reaching the door and crowding into the packed and overflowing theatre. Men and women of fashion and of letters talked of nothing else but the great Garrick and his wonderful Richard. The actor at once rose to the distinction of meriting and receiving the criticism of Walpole, the praise of Pope, and the social attentions of Chesterfield. It was in the character of Richard III. that Garrick first achieved celebrity, and in this character he increased to the end the unfading laurels of his histrionic fame. The morning after his debut in ' Richard III.' his reception was acknowledged by the press to have been "the most extraordinary and great that was ever known on such an occasion." Macklin declared that this was one of the characters in which "the little fellow" secured his own immortality. Mrs. Elizabeth Montague wrote at the time : —

"On Saturday, I intend to go to Goodman's Fields to see Garrick act Richard the Third, that I may get one cold from a regard to sense, I have sacrificed enough to folly, in catching colds at the great puppet-shows in town."

When Pope went to hear Garrick he carried with him a strong prejudice for Betterton's style, which was dignified but stagy, mouthing, and declamatory, while Garrick's style was most natural both in action and in elocution. Pope was captured at once, and, to the intense satisfaction of the actor, applauded with the applauding house. Garrick seems to have been as deeply moved that night by the presence and approbation of Pope as Pope was by the acting of Garrick, for the actor says: —

"When I was told that Pope was in the house, I instantly felt a palpitation at my heart, a tumultuous, not a disagreeable emotion in my mind. I was then in the prime of youth, and in the zenith of my theatrical ambition. It gave me a peculiar pleasure that *Richard* was my character when Pope was to see me and hear me. As I opened my part I saw our little poetical hero dressed in black, seated in a side box near the stage, and viewing me with a serious and earnest attention. His look shot and thrilled like lightning through my frame, and I had some hesitation in proceeding from anxiety and from joy. As *Richard* gradually blazed forth the house was in a roar of applause, and the conspiring hand of Pope shadowed me with laurels."

To know what impression Garrick made on Pope, listen to his euthusiastic eulogy: —

"That young man never had his equal as an actor, and he will never have a rival."

When Garrick acted this part to Peg Woffington's Lady Anne in Dublin, in 1742, the town went mad, and so powerful was Garrick's acting that "women shrieked at Richard's death."

Garrick had a handsome face, capable of marvellous expression, full of animation and intelligence. His general physical proportions were neither great nor inferior, but were all grace and nobleness. His voice was full, rich, and commanding, and capable of expressing every emotion of the heart. In style he was himself alone, and hence the founder of a new school of acting. He was natural, versatile, and intellectual. No quality of an actor seemed wanting in him, with the possible exception of stature. He was qualified in body and mind, in genius and art, to give the theatrical world such a Richard as it had not looked upon since the famous days of Burbage. Walpole pronounced it "as perfect as could be."

Dr. Doran has given us as fine and perhaps as accurate a description of Garrick in the part of Richard as may be found: —

"From the moment the new actor appeared they saw a Richard and not an actor of that personage. Of the audience he seemed unconscious, so thoroughly did he identify himself with the character. He surrendered himself

THE HISTRIONIC RICHARDS.

to all its requirements, was ready for every phase of passion, every change of humor, and was as wonderful in quiet sarcasm as he was terrific in the hurricane of the battle scenes. Above all, his audiences were delighted with his 'nature.' Since Betterton's death, actors had fallen into a rhythmical, mechanical, sing-song cadence. Garrick spoke not as an orator, but as King Richard himself might have spoken. The chuckling exultation of "So much for Buckingham!" was long a tradition on the stage. His 'points' occurred in rapid succession. The rage and rapidity with which he delivered

> 'Cold friends to me! What do they in the North, When they should serve their sovereign in the West?'

made a wonderful impression on the audience. Hogarth has shown us how he *looked*, when starting from his dream; and critics tell us that his cry of 'Give me another horse!' was the cry of a gallant man; but that it fell into one of distress as he said, 'Bind up my wounds,' while the 'Have mercy, Heaven,' was moaned on bended knee. The battle scene and death excited the enthusiasm of an audience altogether unused to acting like this."

Other "points" by which he would electrify an audience were, his hurling away the Prayer Book after he had, with the bishops, closed his conference with the mayor and citizens; his wild, terrified start from sleep in the tent; the desperation with which he fought in the battle scene; the terrible exhibition of will and determination in the death scene, where his hands would convulsively clutch the sod and his fingers dig into the very earth. The impetuosity, suddenness, and terrific energy of action at every climax of tragic interest made the entire performance one of the most remarkable in the history of the stage.

The impression which Garrick made upon the tragic nature of Mrs. Siddons in his performance of Richard has been recorded in the 'Life of John Taylor,' and is valuable in proportion as Mrs. Siddons was a judge of great tragedy. Taylor says:—

"Speaking of Garrick, once when the subject of acting was introduced in company with Mrs. Siddons, I observed so long a time had passed since she saw him act, that perhaps she had forgotten him; on which she said emphatically, it was impossible to forget him. Another time I told her that Mr. Sheridan had declared Garrick's Richard to be very fine, but did not think it terrible enough. 'God bless me!' said she, 'what could be more terrible?' She then informed me, that when she was rehearsing the part of *Lady Anne* to his *Richard*, he desired her, as he drew near her from the couch, to follow him step by step, for otherwise he should be obliged to turn his face from the audience, and he acted much with his features. Mrs. Siddons promised to attend to his desire, but assured me there was such an expression in his acting that it entirely overcame her, and she was obliged to pause, when he gave her such a look of reprehension as she never could recollect without terror."

If he owed much to Ryan for the merits of his Richard, it is Garrick's glory that all subsequent representations have been considered great in proportion as they have approximated the marvellous excellences of his performance.

During Garrick's supremacy several actors entered the field to rival him even in the character of Richard. Aaron Hill in 1744 wrote to his friend Mallet that he had heard Garrick in Macbeth and was highly pleased :

"He is natural, impressed, and easy; has a voice articulate, and placid: his gesture never turbulent, and often well adapted; is untouched by affectation. His peculiar talent lies in pensively preparatory attitudes; whereby, awakening expectation in the audience, he secures and holds fast their attention. . . . I intend to see him quite through *Richard*, — where I have been told, he is thought strongest. I design to see, too, Mr. *Quin*, who has, they say, gone new and noble lengths, in the same character. And, when I have observed them both, you shall have my opinion, very frankly."

Thus Quin was considered a rival of Garrick; but, though he was the Falstaff of his day, his "new and noble lengths" in the character of Richard never brought him into decent comparison with Garrick.

Two very respectable Richards appeared, however, in the performances of Thomas Sheridan and Henry Mossop. Richard III. was Sheridan's first and Mossop's second character. When Sheridan made his debut in Dublin as Richard, he was as much of a sensation in the Irish capital as Garrick had been in the English metropolis. He was young and handsome, gifted with a natural grace, a mellow voice, and a fine intellect. He had the genius and ability successfully to rival Garrick in King John, which actually created jealousy in the bosom of the monarch of the stage. Mossop was an actor of intelligence and college training; he had a finely proportioned body of medium stature, and a voice of great compass, full, rich, and melodious, well adapted to tragedy. He rivalled Garrick in Othello, as Sheridan did in King

John, but he could not win very bright laurels in Richard in competition with the "little fellow." Mossop and Sheridan were rivals, and public sentiment was about evenly divided on the question as to which should stand second only to Garrick in the character of Richard. Mossop's performance is remembered more for its eccentricities than its real merits. His elocution was almost ludicrously deliberate, his gestures were very awkward, and his dress, singular to relate, was white satin puckered!

After Garrick, the next truly great Richard to appear, was that erratic genius, George Frederick Cooke, who made his debut at Covent Garden Theatre, Oct. 31, 1800, in the tragedy of 'Richard III.' His performance immediately established his reputation as an actor of the first rank. The stage had seen no Richard to compare with Cooke's since the brilliant days of Garrick, and even the memory of that great actor's powers did not cast a shadow over Cooke's splendid representation. Cooke had the advantage of having seen Garrick in this his most celebrated character; and it held him in good stead, for there can be no doubt that he followed Garrick in certain "points." His acting in Richard produced a sensation. He wrote of the reception which he received:—

"Never was a reception so flattering. Never did I receive more encouraging, indulgent and warm approbation than that night, both through the play and at the conclusion."

His first play in America was 'Richard III.,' in which he appeared at the Park Theatre, New York, Nov. 21, 1810. It was considered the greatest performance that had ever been seen on the American stage. Richard was Cooke's most celebrated character; he became identified with it in the public mind as Betterton did with Hamlet, Macklin with Shylock, Henderson with Falstaff, Barry with Othello, Kemble with Coriolanus, and Macready with Virginius. As Doran said of Garrick, so may it be said of Cooke, he was Richard, not a mere actor of that personage. In his interesting "Reminiscences," Henry Crabb Robinson in speaking of Cooke says:

"We were so lucky as to see him in *Richard*, his favorite character. Nature has assisted him greatly in the performance of this part, his features being strongly marked and his voice harsh. I felt at the time that he personated the ferocious tyrant better than Kemble could have done."

Leigh Hunt declared that Cooke was for some time the greatest performer of Richard. This opinion was held for a time by Macready, who said, "He was the Richard of his day." And further, Macready says: —

"My remembrance of George Frederick Cooke, whose peculiarities added much to the effect of his performance, served to detract from my confidence in assuming the crooked back tyrant. Cooke's varieties of tone seemed limited to a loud harsh croak descending to the lowest audible murmur; but there was such significance in each inflection, look, and gesture, and such impressive earnestness in his whole bearing, that he compelled your attention and interest."

Again, in speaking of this same performance, Macready says: —

"Cooke's representation of the part I have been present at several times, and it lived in my memory in all its sturdy vigor. I use this expression as applicable to him in the character which Cibber's clever stagy compilation has given to an English audience as 'Richard Plantagenet,' in place of Shakespeare's creation — the earnest, active, versatile spirit, '*impiger, iracundus, inexorabilis, acer*,' who makes a business of his ambition, without let or demur clearing away or cutting down the obstacles to his progress, with not one pause of compunctious hesitation. There was a solidity of deportment and manner, and at the same time a sort of unctuous enjoyment of his successful craft, in the soliloquizing stage villainy of Cooke, which gave powerful and rich effect to the sneers and overbearing retorts of Cibber's hero, and certain points (as the peculiar mode of delivering a passage is technically phrased) traditional from Garrick were made with consummate skill, significance and power."

Leslie pronounced Cooke "the best *Richard* since Garrick;" and C. M. Young "considered him without a rival" in that character. John Howard Payne gives us his impressions of this great actor as he first appeared on the American stage in the tragedy of 'Richard III. :' —

"As regards Cooke, I was at the first performance of Cooke in America. He made a different impression upon me from any other actor I have ever seen; there was something so exclusively unique and original in his dramatic genius. He always presented himself to me in the light of a discoverer, one with whom it seemed that every action and every look emanated entirely from himself; one who appeared never to have had a model, and who depended entirely upon himself for everything he did in the character he represented. Cooke reminds me of no one but himself, and I have never been able to recognize the real *Richard* in any other actor than Cooke."

This opinion has great force when it is known that Payne was intimate with Kean, whom many considered to be the greatest Richard that had ever lived, not even excepting Garrick.

Cooke was, as Robinson intimates, remarkably well adapted to this character by nature. He possessed a manly figure of medium stature, a noble and intellectual face, with a high broad forehead, a prominent nose, an expressive mouth, a strong chin, and splendid, dark, fiery eyes. His features, however, wore a naturally proud, sarcastic, and even sneering expression. His arms were very short, and were used with little regard to the rules of graceful gesture; yet this very natural defect, added to the awkwardness of his gait and motion, made his performance of the crooked-back Richard all the more impressive. He had two voices: one was bitter, harsh, croaking; and the other mild, smooth, and persuasive. In his playing of Richard he would make rapid transitions from one voice to the other with singular and startling effect. Leigh Hunt gives us one of the secrets of Cooke's power in Richard when he says : —

"Mr. Cooke is, in fact, master of every species of hypocrisy. He is great in the most impudent hypocrisy, such as that of Sir Pertinax MacSycophant and of Richard III."

It was this natural sarcasm, this haughty, cynical disposition, that enabled Cooke to play the first three acts of 'Richard III.' with a power peculiar to himself. Though he took his cue from Garrick, he did not seem, like that great actor, to have made his most telling points in the tent scene and in the battle scene. It was in those scenes which called for cunning, hypocrisy, and villany, that he excelled, — not in the scenes of greatest energy of action, but in those where words and looks are most significant. According to Dunlap, Cooke's "superiority over all other Richards" was acknowledged to be "in the dissimulation, the crafty hypocrisy, and the bitter sarcasm of the character." It has been claimed, however, that his craftiness and villany were too apparent. Instead of hiding his cunning and hypocrisy he advertised it in every look and gesture, and every intonation of his voice. His acting was considered strong but coarse, forcible but almost too brutal. And yet his representation in the opinion of play-goers must have been original, thrilling, superb. When he stepped before the footlights of old Park Theatre for the first time, he was fifty-four years old, and his constitution was badly shattered by intemperance; yet, says Dunlap his biographer, "his appearance was picturesque and proudly noble, his head elevated, his step firm, his eye beaming fire." Cooke was as great in the wooing scene with Lady Anne as Garrick was in the tent scene. All the arts and powers of sarcasm, "wheedling flattery," hypocritical humility, cunning suavity, velvet-tongued villany, were brought into play; and such a piece of consummate acting had rarely if ever before been seen. One of the most sensational "points" in the acting of Cooke and Garrick was made with this line which Shakespeare did not write, but which Cibber interpolated into his "adaptation,"—

"Off with his head — so much for Buckingham."

Cooke was original and sensational, if not correct, in pronouncing these words very deliberately, as he stood swaying backward and forward. Other actors, including Garrick, have spoken them in hot haste, and have characterized this whole part of the messenger scene with rapidity and impetuosity of feeling rather than with Cooke's cool, sardonic deliberation. No actor has represented in the character of Richard greater villany and contemptible hypocrisy with less kingliness and heroism than Cooke. In Garrick's performance one of the most striking features was, not the diabolical plotting and planning of murders, the cunning, oily-tongued flattery and insinuation, but rather the courageous, desperate, almost heroic fight and death on Bosworth field. Cooke could not leave this same impression; his mean, cunning, devilish murderer of women and children, his sneering, flattering, hypocritical Richard, could not fight gloriously. He who was so incomparably mean, detestable, fawning, dog-like, in the presence of Lady Anne could not be gallant and manly in the presence of Richmond. Cooke could not act the heroic. He had not the heroic element in his own nature. And it is significantly true that not a single noble-souled, large-hearted, generous man has been able to bring to the stage a great representation of Richard, if exception be made of Burbage, whose personal character is too slightly known to be criticised. It may be claimed that Garrick was an exception; but it will be found that Garrick was one of the most envious, self-conceited, and mean-souled actors of his day, though in his histrionic supremacy he could have afforded to be most generous and great-hearted. Cooke was proud, overbearing, insolent, cynical, drunken, and misanthropic, possessed of a genius which might have found expression in deeds of personal villany had it not found an outlet, a vent, upon the stage in the character of Richard III.

John Philip Kemble was the founder of a school which emphasized the dignified, ornate, scholarly, and graceful in acting, — a school to which have belonged such artists, if not geniuses, as J. P. Kemble, Charles Kemble, C. M. Young, W. C. Macready, Thomas Cooper, Lawrence Barrett, and Henry Irving.

Kemble and Cooke were contemporaries and jealous rivals. Their methods, however, were dissimilar; and as a consequence, there were characters in which each excelled the other. Kemble's Coriolanus, Hamlet, and Macbeth were superior to Cooke's; but his Richard, like his Sir Giles Overreach, "came not within a hundred miles of Cooke." Kemble would not act Richard after he had seen Cooke's performance. There were, however, excellences in Kemble's representation that would have made it popular had it not been for the greater representation of his rival.

Kemble was a solid, dignified, and graceful actor, who sought to produce a great whole, an evenly balanced and harmonious representation. He did not attempt by sudden and unexpected bursts of passion to gain applause. He would not sacrifice the symmetry and dramatic proportions of a play to a few startling and original "points." If he did not possess Cooke's genius, he was admired for a sober judgment, a refined taste, a nobility of mind, and a general culture and art of manner and method which were not found in Cooke. Kemble was a man of splendid physical proportions, his bearing was manly and dignified, his features were handsome and noble, every movement of his body was grace; but he lacked voice and spirit. Though every representation of his was marked by sincerity, taste, and careful study, yet it was often cold, hard, and unimpassioned. Hence he who was superb in Coriolanus could make no very profound impression in Richard III. That character, however, received at his hands an interpretation which was very satisfactory to some critics. Kemble preceded Cooke in this character, and was embarrassed by the memory of Garrick, as he was the first, with the unimportant exception of Henderson, to suffer comparison with him. Kemble's representation possessed the merit of originality. Cooke took his cue from Garrick; had he attempted an original representation he might have created less of a sensation. The physical beauty and noble proportions of Kemble were out of harmony with the deformity of Richard, and as Sir Walter Scott remarks, "from the noble effect of his countenance and figure, neither could he seem constitutionally villanous; he could never *look* the part of Richard, and it seemed a jest to hear him, whose countenance and person were so eminently fine, descant on his own deformity." Kemble was not endowed with that bitter, misanthropic, sneering disposition, which held Cooke and Kean in good stead in the character of Richard. He lacked also the energy, which he sacrificed to grace, to fill the whole stage with the desperate, vehement, terrible action of the usurper. He could not, or would not, rise to the climaxes of "dreadful energy" which characterized Garrick's performance, nor work up to the "frightful passion " of a Junius Brutus Booth. He lacked force, intensity, and action.

There were, notwithstanding these faults, certain marked and valuable characteristics in Kemble's representation which will forever preserve it from inferiority, if they do not elevate it above mediocrity. While in the acting of Garrick, Cooke, Kean, and Booth, the villany of Richard was apparent in every gesture, look, and intonation, in Kemble's artistic representation it was covered up by a semblance of virtue and nobility. Kemble's Richard did not advertise his diabolism on all his features, nor proclaim it in all his vocal inflections. This dignified actor used to argue, as Scott says, "that Richard III., being of high descent and breeding, ought not to be vulgar in his appearance, or coarse in his cruelty." And Scott intimates that Kemble incorrectly gave to Richard not only "a tinge of aristocracy," but represented him to be "of a generous and chivalrous character" and a "handsome prince." This representation was relieved of the uninterrupted darkness and terror of Cooke's and Garrick's performances. There came in upon those horrible scenes occasional rays of light through Kemble's interpretation, which not a few welcomed, not only as original, but as correct and artistic. It is singular, however, that two critics of ability can study a performance of this character and disagree as to what merits it lacks or possesses. Charles Lamb admired certain features of Kemble's Richard, and lamented that "the sportive relief which he threw into the darker shades of Richard disappeared with him." Lamb saw the "sportive relief" of Kemble's performance. Henry Crabb Robinson says, in speaking of Cooke's performance: "I felt at the time that he personated the ferocious tyrant better than Kemble could have done. There is besides a sort of humor in his acting which appeared very appropriate, and which I think Kemble could not have given." Robinson saw "a sort of humor" in Cooke's Richard, but could not, like Lamb, see it in Kemble's. In the wooing of Lady Anne, Kemble was weak, as he was in the closing scenes of the tragedy; that is to say, his faults were in scenes which demand great hypocrisy and villany, and in scenes of impetuosity and rush of action. He excelled in the soliloquies of the play, and in scenes where there is a demand for dignity and princely bearing.

As Cooke and Kemble were waning, there flashed upon the English stage the light of a new and incomparable genius, — Edmund Kean. It is doubtful whether a greater Richard was ever seen. No traditions of Burbage or Garrick were able to cast his wonderful performance into shade. It was perhaps the most original, and in all its parts the most wonderful, representation that had appeared since the days of Burbage and Shakespeare.

Cooke followed Garrick, and some have charged that Kean imitated Cooke. This last charge is without foundation; for greatly as Kean admired the genius of Cooke, he once told John Howard Payne that he had never seen that actor in the character of Richard. Kean's performance seems to have combined the excellences of both Garrick and Cooke. Kean and Cooke were very similar in natural disposition, in moral make-up. They were both haughty, cynical, egotistic, coarse, intemperate, and uncontrollably passionate and misanthropic. They were similarly endowed with power to represent cunning, villany, hypocrisy, and brutal cruelty. Neither of these actors had a fine, melodious voice to be compared with a Garrick's or a Young's. Yet their voices did not lack power, but possessed the quality, which may be used with great effect in Richard, of transition from the harsh, croaking, and bitter to the smooth, mellow, and insinuating tones. Kean's physical qualifications were inferior in many respects to Cooke's, and also to Kemble's and Garrick's. He was insignificant in stature; he shuffled in his gait. He had not Cooke's expanse of brow, strength of chin, and general nobility of feature. Yet he had a wonderful eye, full, black, and intense; and though his features were not cast in a noble mould, they possessed marvellous powers of expression, so that no actor could *look* Richard more perfectly than Kean. To this power to *look* Richard Kean added the power to *act* him; herein he surpassed Kemble. Though he was fitted for the part in natural temperament, Kean possessed less natural acrimony and meanness than Cooke, and may have fallen behind that actor in those scenes where this spirit is expressed; yet he had a more impetuous, nervous, magnetic nature, which enabled him to excel Cooke in energy and terrific force of action, and in power to electrify an audience by sudden and magnificent outbursts of passion. Cooke's genius was more limited in its range than Kean's. While the former is remembered more for his Richard than for any other Shakespearian character he assumed, Kean is remembered for his greatness in Shylock and Othello as well as in Richard. The general verdict seems to accord to Kean the superiority even in Richard. Cooke, no doubt, was incomparable in certain scenes; but, taking the whole tragedy into consideration, Kean's was the greater Richard. Cooke was not known in his character of Richard before his forty-fifth year, when he made his debut at Covent Garden; but Kean's performance in this character may be traced back to his boyhood. He was a life-long actor of the part. We are indebted to C. M. Young for one of our first glimpses of Kean's Richard. The boy, with his mother, Nance Carey, was strolling about the country giving exhibitions of his histrionic precocity, when one day about the Christmas time he chanced to bring up at the door of Thomas Young's hospitable mansion, and was admitted to the hall, where Charles Young first saw him. Evidently the elder Young had planned a little entertainment for the boy and friends who had come to enjoy one of his delightful dinners, and at the proper time the genial host " ordered the butler to bring in ' the boy.' "

"On his entry he was taken by the hand, patted on the head, and requested to favor the company with a specimen of his histrionic ability. With a self-possession marvellous in one so young he stood forth, knitted his brow, hunched up one shoulder-blade, and, with sardonic grin and husky voice, spouted forth Gloster's opening soliloquy in Richard III. He then recited selections from some of our minor British poets, both grave and gay; danced a hornpipe; sang songs, both comic and pathetic; and, for fully an hour, displayed such versatility, as to elicit vociferous applause from his auditory, and substantial evidence of its sincerity by a shower of crown pieces and shillings — a napkin having been opened and spread upon the floor for their reception. The accumulated treasures having been poured into the gaping pockets of the lad's trousers, with a smile of gratified vanity and grateful acknowledgment, he withdrew, . . . and left the house rejoicing. The door was no sooner closed than every one present desired to know the name of the youthful prodigy who had so astonished them. The host replied, that this was not the first time he had had him to amuse his friends; that he knew nothing of the lad's history or antecedents; but that his name was Edmund Kean."

Dr. Young spoke a good word for tne wonderful boy whenever opportunity offered, and recommended him to Mrs. Clarke, who finally met him with the kindly question, "Are you the little boy who can act so well?" Edmund having answered with a polite bow, the good lady further asked, "What can you act?" Without hesitation he answered, "Richard the Third, Speed the Plough, Hamlet, and Harlequin." "I should like to see you act," said the lady in admiration. "I," replied he with flushed cheeks, "should be proud to act to you." Arrangements were made for an appearance. The boy in the character of Richard astonished his auditors. All were enthusiastic in his praise, and Mrs. Clarke took him under her care to educate him for the stage.

Kean had done his rehearsing or practising in the character of Richard in a garret over a London bookstore. At the early age of fourteen he was on the stage. When engaged at Drury Lane Theatre in children's parts, he attracted the attention of notable actors and actresses by his spontaneous outbursts of tragic declamation in the green-room. On one occasion Mrs. Charles Kemble asked who was creating the disturbance, when some one replied: "It is little Carey [Kean] reciting 'Richard III.' after the manner of Garrick; go and see him, he is really very clever." When, later in his career, Kean acted this part in the provincial towns of Ireland and England, he met with little success. Though in his representation there was rising the greatest Richard of the modern stage, the play-goers could not appreciate it, and while they were delighted with his ballads and jigs they nodded over his wonderful performance of 'Richard III.' He was hissed on one occasion because he forgot the audience in his complete absorption in the part; and for their ignorant boorish manners, Kean stepped to the front of the stage and shouted, "Unmannered dogs! Stand ye, when I command!" It awed the "unmannered dogs" to silence.

When Kean appeared at Drury Lane in 1814, at the age of thirty-one, the manager requested him to make his debut in 'Richard III.;' but the actor was too sensitive about his physical inferiority, and shrank from appearing in a part which would place him at a disadvantage on account of his slight stature. He therefore insisted upon appearing as Shylock, in which he achieved unquestioned success. With the encouragement of this triumph he ventured to appear in the character of Richard. He had almost if not quite wrested the sceptre from Macklin as Shylock; in 'Richard III.' he had to contend against the splendid traditions of Garrick and Cooke. He succeeded at least in sharing, if not in fully capturing, their laurels. His Richard at Drury Lane in 1815 was as great a hit as Garrick's at Goodman's Fields in 1741. As it was with that famous actor, so was it with Kean, "the town became his own."

Pope eulogized Garrick, and Byron went wild over Kean. The prophecy of Beverley, the Cheltenham manager, was fulfilled in about two years after it was generously uttered. Oxberry tells us that when the loafers who hissed Kean's Richard from the Cheltenham stage blamed Beverley for "suffering such a creature to do Richard," the wary manager replied: "That creature in a few years will be the greatest creature in the metropolis, and you will go far and near to get a glimpse of him." On the night of Feb. 12, 1815, Edmund Kean as 'Richard III.' was "the greatest creature in the metropolis;" nay, the greatest creature in the histrionic world. That first performance has been well described

by H. B. Baker, in his interesting work on
"Our Old Actors:" —

"He approached the part with fear and trembling. 'I am so frightened,' he said before the curtain rose, 'that my acting will be almost dumb show to-night.' But nevertheless, from the first soliloquy to the appalling last scene, he took both audience and critics by storm. The performance must have been wonderfully like Garrick's. . . . Mrs. Garrick, who went to see him play it, told Dibdin that Cooke put her in mind of her husband, but Kean was like Garrick himself."

Dr. Doran has given us a striking sketch of Kean's triumph on that memorable occasion: —

"A few nights before he played the part, it was performed at Covent Garden, by John Kemble; and a short time after Kean had triumphed it was personated by Young; but Kemble could not prevent, nor Young impede, the triumph of the new actor, who now made Richard his own, as he had previously done with Shylock.

"His Richard (on the 12th of February) settled his position with the critics; and the criticism to which he was subjected was, for the most part, admirably and impartially written. He is sometimes spoken of as 'this young man;' at others, 'this young gentleman.'

'Even Cooke's performance,' says one, 'was left at an immeasurable distance.' A second adds, 'it was the most perfect performance of any that has been witnessed since the days of Garrick.' Of the grand effects followed by a storm of applause, a third writes that 'electricity itself was never more instantaneous in its operation.'"

Lord Byron was more enthusiastic over Kean's performance than Pope over Garrick's. He went to his room and wrote in his diary: —

"Just returned from seeing Kean in Richard. By Jove, he is a soul! Life, nature, truth, without exaggeration or diminution. Kemble's *Hamlet* is perfect, but *Hamlet* is not Nature. *Richard* is a man; and Kean is *Richard*."

Kean's "points" in this representation were numerous. Oxberry's criticism furnishes us with one of them: —

"In his opening soliloquy of Richard, which has been pronounced to be unequalled, he commits a glaring error, by pausing after the words 'And my first step shall be,' — as if Richard had not previously determined that it should be, — 'on Henry's head.'"

This "point" was made with one of Cibber's interpolations.

In the wooing scene with Lady Anne, his acting was considered most original and artistic, though his hypocrisy and scorn have been criticised as too apparent and too coarse. Henry Crabb Robinson has given us his impressions of Kean's great performance: —

"He played *Richard*, I believe, better than any man I ever saw; yet my expectations were pitched too high, and I had not the pleasure I expected. The expression of malignant joy is the one in which he surpasses all men I have ever seen. And his most flagrant defect is want of dignity. His face is finely expressive, though his mouth is not handsome, and he projects his lower lip ungracefully; yet it is finely suited to *Richard*. He gratified my eye more than my ear. . . . His declamation is very unpleasant, but my ear may in time be reconciled to it, as the palate is to new cheese and tea. It often reminds me of Blanchard's. His speech is not fluent, and his words and syllables are too distinctly separated. His finest scene was with Lady Anne, and his mode of lifting up her veil to watch her countenance was exquisite. The concluding scene was unequal to my expectation, though the fencing was elegant, and his sudden death fall was shockingly real."

Kean made a fine "point" out of the lines, —

"He did corrupt frail nature with a bribe,
To shrink my arm up like a wither'd shrub."

He would look for some time with contempt at the puny arm, and then slap it in anger and mortification out of his sight. It will be noticed that the lines with which Kean made this fine and startling point do not belong to Shakespeare's play of 'Richard III.,' but are Colley Cibber's interpolation from 'Henry VI.' We are again indebted to Doran for a fine enumeration of Kean's "points" in this representation : —

"Joyous and sarcastic in the opening soliloquy; devilish, as he passed his bright sword through the still breathing body of Lancaster; audaciously hypocritical, and almost too exulting, in the wooing of Lady Anne; cruelly kind to the young Princes, his eye smiling while his foot seemed restless to crush the two spiders that so vexed his heart; — in representing all this there was an originality and a nature which were entirely new to the delighted audience. Then they seemed to behold altogether a new man revealed to them, in the first words uttered by him from the throne, — 'Stand all apart!' from which period to the last struggle with Richmond, there was an uninterrupted succession of beauties; even in the by-play he found means to extort applause, and a graceful attitude, an almost silent chuckle, a significant glance, — even so common-place a phrase as 'good night, my lords,' uttered before the battle of the morrow, were responded to by acclamations such as are awarded to none but the great masters of the art."

Macready was particularly impressed with Kean's wooing of Lady Anne, his interview with Buckingham when he proposed the murder of the two young Princes, and with the terrible energy with which he hurried every plan to execution. While he admired Cooke in certain parts more than Kean, he gave to the latter higher praise for his representation as a whole. It was Macready's opinion that Kean never displayed more masterly elocution than in the third act of 'Richard III.'

Hazlitt was an enthusiastic admirer of Kean in the character of Richard, declaring that "we cannot imagine any character represented with greater distinctness and precision, more perfectly *articulated* in every part." This able critic notes, among others, the following "points:" —

"He is more refined than Cooke, more bold, varied, and original than Kemble in the same character. . . . The courtship scene with Lady Anne is an admirable exhibition of smooth and smiling villainy. . . . Mr. Kean's attitude in leaning against the side of the stage before he comes forward to address Lady Anne, is one of the most graceful and striking ever witnessed on the stage. It would do for Titian to paint. . . . His by-play is excellent. His manner of bidding his friends 'Good night,' after pausing with the point of his sword, drawn slowly backward and forward on the ground, as if considering the plan of the battle next day, is a particularly happy and natural thought. He gives to the two last acts of the play the greatest animation and effect. He fills every part of the stage. . . . The concluding scene in which he is killed by Richmond is the most brilliant of the whole. He fights at last like one drunk with wounds ; and the attitude in which he stands with his hands stretched out, after his sword is wrested from him, has a preternatural and terrific grandeur, as if his will could not be disarmed, and the very phantoms of his despair had power to kill."

Sir Walter Scott gives us a glimpse of one of Kean's "points" in acting when he refers to "the drunken and dizzy fury with which Richard, as personated by Kean, continues to make the motion of striking after he has lost his weapon."

To refer again to the ever-enjoyable Doran, we find this picture of the closing scene, made the more interesting by anecdote : —

"The triumph was cumulative, and it was crowned by the tent scene, the battle, and the death. Probably no actor ever even approached Kean in the two last incidents. He fenced with consummate grace and skill, and fought with an energy that seemed a fierce reality. Rae had sneered at the 'little man,' but Rae now felt bound to be civil to the great tragedian, and referring to the passage of arms in 'Richard III.,' he, having to play Richmond, asked, 'Where shall I hit you, sir, to-night?' 'Where you can, sir,' answered Kean; and he kept Richmond off, in that famous struggle, till Rae's sword-arm was weary with making passes. His attempt to 'collar' Richmond when his own sword had fallen from him was so doubtful in taste that he subsequently abandoned it; but in the faint, yet deadly-meant passes, which he made with his swordless arm, after he had received his death-blow, there was the conception of a great artist; and there died with him a malignity which mortal man had never before so terribly portrayed."

One feature of this last scene, of great force and interest, Talfourd refers to in his criticism :—

"His last look at *Richmond* as he stands is fearful; as if the agony of death gave him power to menace his conqueror with the ghostly terrors of the world into which the murderous tyrant is entering."

Kean made his first appearance in America on the 8th of January, 1821; he made his debut in 'Richard III.,' as Cooke had done about ten years previously. The Philadelphia theatre was crowded to excess, and he was received with the most rapturous applause, as was the case with Cooke at the New York theatre in 1810. It is doubtful whether Kean succeeded in wresting the sceptre from Cooke, who had made a wonderful fame in America. The 'Democratic Press' voiced the universal verdict as to the greatness of Kean in the last scene of 'Richard III.:' —

"So much had been said of the dying scenes of Mr. Kean, that curiosity was at its *topmost round* when the fight began, *which was to issue* in his death. All that we had heard, — all that we could ever hear, on this head, must necessarily fall infinitely short of the extraordinary powers displayed by Mr. Kean in the last scene. He writhed with bodily pain; *he agonized* under the terrors of conscience; he *gasped* for breath; his every motion evinced distress, and approaching death, *his* sufferings were so painful to the beholder, that *he* felt relieved when nature was exhausted and *Richard* had expired."

One or two very good anecdotes are related of Kean in connection with his celebrated and incomparable representation of Richard III., showing that the admiration of some was not founded on an independent judgment or study of his characterization, and also showing that all persons did not look upon him as the greatest Richard. On the authority of F. Reynolds, a rising and self-conscious barrister on one occasion, in company with quite a number of political and literary notables, took occasion to compliment Kean by saying —

"that he had never seen acting until the preceding evening. 'Indeed!' said Kean; 'why you must have seen others, sir, I should conceive, in *Richard III.*' 'I have seen,' replied the barrister, 'both Cooke and Kemble; but they must excuse me, Mr. Kean, if I should turn from them, and frankly say to you, with *Hamlet,* "Here's metal more attractive."' Kean felt highly flattered. The conversation then turning on a curious lawsuit, Kean, after a pause, asked the barrister if he had ever visited the Exeter Theatre. 'Very rarely indeed,' was the reply, 'though, by the by, now I recollect, during the last assizes, I dropped in towards the conclusion of Richard III. *Richmond* was in the hands of a very promising young fellow; but such a *Richard!* — such a harsh, croaking, barn brawler! I forget his name, but' — 'I 'll tell it you,' interrupted the Drury Lane hero, rising and tapping the great lawyer on the shoulder: 'I'll tell it you — *Kean.*'"

'Blackwood's Magazine' is responsible for the following story : —

"During one of Charles Kean's visits to the United States, he was entertained at dinner by one of the great New York merchants. Opposite to him at the table there sat a gentleman, who continued to observe him with marked attention, and at last called on the host to present him to Mr. Kean. The introduction was duly made, and ratified by drinking wine together; when the stranger, with much impressiveness of manner, said, 'I saw you in Richard last night:' Kean, feeling, not unnaturally, that a compliment was approaching, smiled blandly and bowed. 'Yes, sir,' continued the other, in a slow, almost judicial tone, 'I have seen your father in Richard; and I saw the late Mr. Cooke' — another pause, in which Charles Kean's triumph was gradually mounting higher and higher. 'Yes, sir; Cooke, sir, was better than your father; and your father, sir, a long way better than you!'"

Fanny Kemble, rising above the prejudices of her own education, could with womanly generosity and intelligence write : —

"Kean is gone, and with him are gone Othello, Shylock, and Richard. . . . Who that ever saw will ever forget the fascination of his dying eyes in *Richard*, when deprived of his sword; the wondrous power of his look seemed yet to avert the uplifted arm of Richmond. If he was irregular and unartisticlike in his performance, so is *Niagara* compared with the waterworks of Versailles."

It is said that an hour before his death Kean sprang from his couch crying, as Richard, —

" A horse, a horse, my kingdom for a horse ! "

Charles Kean, though " the son of his father," was not a chip of the old block. He attempted to follow in the footsteps of Edmund Kean, and doubtless made his great mistake in choosing those parts in which he would necessarily be compared unfavorably with that great genius. He made his American debut in ' Richard III.,' but was not able to create the enthusiasm which attended his father's performance. There seemed to be a prophecy in the words of Edmund Kean when, after acting Richard one night and looking upon a little performance of Charles at home, he said : " The name of Kean shall die with *me.* It shall be buried in my coffin." And it was.

The stage has not seen a great Richard since Kean's day; that is to say, an original, powerful representation, to be compared with Garrick, Cooke, or Kean.

This difficult part has been attempted by nearly every Shakespearian actor, but rarely with pronounced success. Young, Cooper, Phelps, Macready, Forest, and J. B. Booth in the earlier days, and Irving, Lawrence Barrett, Wilson Barrett, and Edwin Booth in recent times, have been the great histrionic interpreters of Shakespeare in England and America. While any one of these may have had, or may have the talent to give a clever and acceptable performance of 'Richard III.,' it is doubtful whether any one of them has had the genius to create a new, original, and great Richard.

Cooper had his admirers, who claimed that Kean alone surpassed him in this character. Young attempted to eclipse Kean's performance, but signally failed, though in certain characters, on account of his physical advantages, he was Kean's superior.

Macready's talent was superior to his genius, yet he must rank with the first of actors. The stage has seldom if ever known a greater Virginius. He performed every part which he undertook intelligently and with scholarly good taste; but he could never rise to the heights of a Garrick, a Cooke, or a Kean in such trying and difficult characters as Othello, Shylock, Lear, and Richard III. Admirers of Macready have claimed that he "determined his position as a first-class actor" by his performance of Richard III. He had seen Kean in this character and greatly admired him, placing him above Cooke. One of Macready's merits was his individuality, independence, and originality. His faults were his own, as were his merits; he aped no other actor. His style was a medium between Kemble and Kean. He did not possess all the excellences of both, but he avoided many of their faults. He was neither as cold as Kemble nor as fervent and magnetic as Kean; yet he had much of the Kemble dignity and scholarly taste, with some measure of the spirit of Kean. His Richard therefore was a representation that must be classed between the too princely Richard of the one and the too villanous Richard of the other.

There was some rivalry between Macready and Kean in this very part, and the critics were not slow to see merits in the new actor which the old favorite did not possess. Leigh Hunt's comparison of these two representations is undoubtedly just, while it gives us a fair estimate of Macready in the character of Richard: —

"Mr. Kean's Richard is the more sombre, perhaps the deeper part of him — Mr. Macready's the livelier and more animal part, a very considerable one nevertheless. Mr. Kean's is the more gloomy and reflective villain, rendered so by the united effects of his deformity and subtle-mindedness; Mr. Macready's is the more ardent and bold-faced one, borne up by a temperament naturally high and sanguine, though pulled down by mortification. The one has more of the seriousness of conscious evil in it, the other of the gaiety of meditated success. Mr. Kean's has gone deeper even than the relief of his conscience, he has found melancholy at the bottom of that necessity for relief; Mr. Macready's is more sustained in his troubled waters by constitutional vigor and buoyancy. In short, Mr. Kean's Richard is more like King Richard darkened by the shadow of his approaching success, and announcing by the depth of his desperation when it shall be disputed; Mr. Macready's Richard is more like the Duke of Glocester, brother to the gay tyrant Edward the Fourth, and partaking as much of his character as the contradictions of the family handsomeness in his person would allow. If these two features in the character of Richard could be united by an actor, the performance would be a perfect one."

Indeed, what a performance that would be, with an actor possessing all the merits and none of the faults of Kean and Macready! But the name of Macready never calls up by association the name of Richard; on the other hand, "Kean" and "Cooke" are almost synonymous with "Richard."

There are not a few who look upon Junius Brutus Booth as the last, but not the least, of the great Richards of the English stage. Booth's fame is almost entirely American. He was not able to sustain himself in competition with Kean in England. He made his debut at Covent Garden, London, in the character of Richard, and also made his first appearance in America in the same character. It is quite excusable in Mr. Edwin Booth that he should think his gifted father had more than half gained the victory over Kean in Richard and Lear, and carelessly threw it away as a trifle. It may be honor enough for Booth that he was a greater Hamlet than Kean or Cooke; it adds nothing to his fame to vainly compare him with either of these geniuses in 'Richard III.' Nothwithstanding this, Richard was one of Booth's favorite and most popular parts, especially in America. This was generally 'his first-night character.

In London, Richmond, New York, Boston, Philadelphia, and Pittsburgh, he first appeared in 'Richard III.' Booth was a follower of Kean, if not a very close and slavish imitator. He may have had genius, but it was a genius without great originality or power of invention. He did not strike out a new line, as did Garrick, Kemble, Kean, and Macready. He was not unlike Kean in temperament. He was an energetic, magnetic, impulsive actor, quite as erratic as Cooke or Kean. He had the natural, physical qualifications for the character of Richard, and in certain parts acted with great power. Booth made his "points" in scenes requiring the greatest action. He was greatest where Kean and Garrick were greatest, and, even in these scenes, reminded his hearers of the geniuses he imitated more than he impressed them with the originality and high order of his own genius. He was not great in the first scenes, where Cooke and Kemble were at their best. There was a magnetism in his voice, a fire in his eye, a significance in his gesture which enabled him at times to get the better of his hearers' judgment, and in spite of tricks and misinterpretations, to carry them away with enthusiasm. Certain critics declared that "his whisper could chill the blood;" "his glance extort obedience;" "his very gesture drew tears." There can be no doubt that Booth was great in the tent scene and battle scene of 'Richard III.' Traditions and the critics seem to agree in pronouncing the fight one of the most terrific and thrilling representations ever witnessed on the stage. The picture may not be overdrawn which Stone gives us in his 'Theatrical Reminiscences:'

"The dying scene of Booth was truly frightful — his eyes, naturally large and piercing, appeared to have greatly increased in size, and fairly gleamed with fire; large drops of perspiration oozed from his forehead, and coursing down his cheeks, mingling with and moistening the ringlets of the wig he usually wore in Richard, caused them to adhere to his face, rendering his appearance doubly horrible. The remarkable portrayal of the passions, — the despair, hate, grief, — in the passage in the original text which reads —

'But the vast renown thou
Hast acquired in conquering
Richard, doth give him more,
Than the soul departing from the body,'

has probably never been surpassed even by George Frederick Cooke, whose Richard is said to have excelled all others."

Mr. Stone would encounter some difficulties in attempting to find the lines quoted above in the original text of Shakespeare's 'Richard III.' But from this bit of reminiscence we learn that Booth, like the other great Richards, made some of his most powerful and celebrated "points" with the Colley Cibber interpolations. Ludlow has given as accurate a description of Booth's representation, as a whole, as may perhaps be found among reminiscences: —

"When the proper scene opened, Mr. Booth walked on the stage, made no recognition of the reception applause, and, in an apparently meditative mood began the soliloquy of 'Now is the winter of our discontent,' which he delivered with seeming indifference, and with little if any point, something after the manner of a schoolboy repeating a lesson of which he had learned the words, but was heedless of their meaning, and then made his exit, without receiving any additional applause. I was not where I could ascertain the impression made upon the audience, but on the stage, at the side scenes, the actors were looking at each other in all kinds of ways, expressive of astonishment and disgust. I was standing near Mr. Benton, an old actor, the *King Henry* of the evening, — and as I turned to go away, he said, 'What do you think of him, Mr. Ludlow?' 'Think,' I replied, 'why, I think as I thought before, that he is an impostor! What do *you* think of him?' 'Why, sir,' said Benton, 'if the remainder of his *Richard* shall prove like the beginning, I have never yet, I suppose, seen the character played, for it is unlike any I ever saw; it may be very good, but I don't fancy it!' . . . I retained my first impression of Mr. Booth until he came to the fourth act, where, in a scene with *Buckingham*, he hints at the murder of the young princes. Then I thought I discovered something worthy of a great actor. From that on, his acting was unique and wonderful. I had never seen any one produce such effects, and come so near my ideas of the character, — not even Mr. Cooke, who was as far below Mr. Booth in the last two acts as he was above him in the first three."

This seems a very fair description and a just comparison. But it does not contradict the claim that Booth was below Cooke in the first three acts, and below Kean in the last two. Cooke was the greatest Richard in the first three acts; Kean the greatest Richard in the last two. Booth was not the greatest Richard in any act, though he may have the fame of standing next to Kean in the parts where Kean was, and is, and doubtless ever will be, first.

The Primrose Criticism merits our thanks for having prompted the fresh investigation, which has strengthened our confidence in the Shakespearian authorship of 'Richard III.' A tragedy so faithful to history, so clearly the climax of a series of plays of common origin, so unified and intensified in one great and terrible character, so universally indorsed as Shakespearian by the poets, critics, antiquarians, and Shakespearian editors of the past three hundred years, so popular with the greatest histrionic geniuses of the English stage, and so worthy of their highest efforts and most glorious triumphs, — such a tragedy is not unworthy of him who

". . . was not of an age, but for all time."

www.ingramcontent.com/pod-product-compliance
Lightning Source LLC
Chambersburg PA
CBHW022119160426
43197CB00009B/1090